The Herb Patch

BY • JANET • VICKERS

[redacted]

First Printing: **October, 1983**
Second Printing: **February, 1990**
Third Printing: **August, 1993**

Published by: **NuYu Enterprises**
a division of NuYu Products Ltd.,
P.O. Box 30234
Calgary, Alberta, Canada T2H 2V9

Designed, Printed and Produced in Canada by:
Centax Books, a Division of PrintWest Ltd.
Publishing Director: Margo Embury
1150 Eighth Avenue
Regina, Saskatchewan, Canada S4R 1C9
(306) 525-2304 Fax (306) 757-2439

ISBN 0-9691888-0-3

Thanks to
Ironmask Antiques, Calgary
Super Plants, Calgary
Campbell Flowers, Calgary

Bibliography

Rose, Jeanne — Herbs and Things — New York, Grosset & Dunlop, 1972.

Vickers, Janet — Basic Herbs and Simple Remedies, Calgary, NuYu Enterprises.

Kloss, Jethro — Back to Eden — Riverside California — Lifeline Books.

Meyer, Joseph E. — The Herbalist, Hammond, [redacted] — Indiana Botanical Gardens.

CONTENTS

NOTICE

The information presented in this book is given as a help to those interested in old remedies and natural herbal therapy. It is not offered as a replacement for your physician or conditions that require his services. It does not promote patent medicines, nutritional preparations or guarantee the effectiveness of any remedy. These simple remedies have been handed down through generations and have been used frequently in our home with success. We present them to you dear reader, that they will enrich and enlighten your homes. Use wisely the natural things of the earth that God has given us.

The Author

ACKNOWLEDGEMENTS

My sincere thanks to Marjorie Burakoff who again gave me useful suggestions as well as enthusiasm. To those people across the country who wrote their appreciation for the first book and encouraged this one. To Hugh my husband who is a loving determined motivator.

OTHER BOOKS BY THE AUTHOR

Basic Herbs and Simple Remedies

INTRODUCTION

From the very beginning, mankind utilized plants both as medicine and food. In order to survive, a knowledge of the plant world was essential. Lessons were learned the hard way — which herbs to use in moderation, if at all, and which others to use to nourish and revitalize the body. How, can herbs revitalize the body? Plants draw their nutrition from the soil; different species each contain certain elements that will produce different results when taken into the human body.

The study of plants and their effects on the human system is what herbology is all about. During the past 20 years there has been a revival of interest in herbs and their uses. People everywhere are studying and experimenting and growing herb gardens. This book just touches on some of the uses of plants, and I might add at this print, there are many not listed here. Because of space limitations, I could not possibly include descriptions of every herb, and so I have chosen to write about those herbs with many and varied uses.

Just because herbs are grown in the soil instead of produced in a lab doesn't mean that caution should be disregarded when using them. Some people may have an allergic reaction to some of them — if so discontinue use and replace with herb of similar action. Do not try treating serious illness yourself — always consult your physician for advice. This book was written to help you discover the use of various plants as simple medicinal aids, beauty treatments and food sources. If nothing else it will give you an appreciation of the creator's handiwork.

The Author.

USE HERBS WITH WISDOM

Since you are studying plants and their effects, there is a need to acquaint yourself with some plants that can be potentially dangerous. Children particularly are vulnerable, especially the very young. The interesting thing is the same herb can be helpful or poisonous depending on how it is taken. When planting a garden take into consideration young children — even if you don't have any, a neighbour's child can wander in and inadvertently eat a plant. The following list contains plants with restrictions on use.

PLANTS — TOXIC EFFECTS

Name of Plant	Toxic Part	Symptons and Notes
Apple Seeds	Seeds in large quantity.	Breathing difficulty, coma.
Azalea	Whole plant.	Low blood pressure, convulsions, vomiting.
Belladonna	Whole plant.	Pupil dilation, paralysis.
Bleeding Heart	Whole plant.	Vomiting, diarrhea, cramps.
Buttercup	Fresh whole plant.	Do not use without supervision
Castor Bean	Whole plant, especially seeds.	Nausea, vomiting, cramps, convulsions (castor oil is not poisonous).
Daffodils	Bulb.	Vomiting, diarrhea, convulsion
Delphiniums	Whole plant.	Nausea, vomiting.
Elderberries	Whole fresh plant. (Not cooked berries).	Nausea, dizziness, diarrhea.
Flax	(unripe seeds)	Use only ripe seeds.
Foxglove	Whole plant.	Diarrhea, vomiting, cramps, convulsions (Use only under medical supervision).
Hellebore	Whole plant.	Same as above.
Henbane	Whole plant, especially the seeds.	Vomiting, cramps, nausea, (primarily for external use)
Holly	(Berries)	Especially dangerous to children.
Horse Chestnuts	Seeds, flowers, leaves, (especially for children).	Diarrhea, cramps, vomiting, paralysis.
Hyacinths	Bulbs	Nausea, cramps, diarrhea.
Lily of the Valley	Whole Plant.	Dizziness, vomiting, sweating (acts like the Foxglove).
Lobelia	(Whole plant if given in overdoses).	Use under medical supervision only.
Milkweed	Roots if taken in large quantities.	Good for external use.
Mistletoe	Berries (poisonous).	Cramps, diarrhea, death.
Nettle	Old raw plants.	Young plants are eaten in salad, old ones can produce poisoning symptoms.
Nutmeg	Seeds (2 can be fatal).	Hallucinations, double vision, delirium, cramps.
Pokeweed	Whole plant.	Vomiting, cramps, convulsion.
Rhubarb	Leaves (the rest of the plant is fine).	Cramps, nausea, vomiting, convulsions, internal bleeding.

A SMALL HERB GARDEN

Once you have decided to grow some herbs in your garden several questions will arise — which ones to choose and for what purpose (medicinal, culinary, or cosmetic or, some of all three). An important consideration is space — this may even influence your original choice. Some herbs are extremely prolific and can overtake a garden area in no time. Many herbs are relatively easy to raise, especially the culinary herbs — they do however seem to enjoy strong sunshine perhaps because many of them originated in the Mediterranean area where they thrived on heat.

Herbs grow to different heights so

care must be taken when planning your garden to place the tall ones to the rear rather than forefront so that other smaller plants can be reached with no difficulty. Accessibility is also important, a culinary herb that is used more often should be planted nearer to your kitchen door so that there is no necessity to trample through your garden to pick something (especially if it's raining and there is considerable mud around). A good idea would be to visit your local nursery garden and actually see some of the layouts used and ask some questions. Most professional gardeners are very willing to share their knowledge with you. Soil preparation is most important — good healthy soil produces plants of the same quality, so a little extra effort in the beginning is well worth the effort. Clay soil needs ashes and sand added to improve conditions. The best soil is on the alkaline side. You may also consider growing some herbs in boxes within your own home.

Above all, enjoy your herb garden, there is something so satisfying and creative about working with nature. Have fun!

Anise

This is an annual plant that grows up to 18 inches high. It is not really suitable for indoor growing because of the long tap root that required sufficient depth of soil. Since it does not transplant too successfully, it is better to start it off where it is to stay. It requires well drained soil conditions and needs to be planted early in the year. Thin plants to 8 inches apart. The gathering of the seeds is best in fall. Anise seeds can be used to flavor cakes, cookies, breads, etc. as well as for digestive upsets. The leaves are especially delicious when used in salads.

Sweet Basil

Basil is an annual that of course has to be raised from seed or seedling each year. This plant loves the sun and a moist soil. When planting seedlings give space of 8 inches apart and be sure to pinch back the centre to create a bushy plant. Basil contains an aromatic oil that is quite strong, so when experimenting remember to use sparingly. It can be grown in containers and taken indoors if desired. Tomato dishes, soups, salads, fish, chicken and cheese are enhanced with a touch of basil.

Burnet

The tender young shoots of this plant give a delicious flavor to most salads. It is a hardy perennial that grows up to 13 inches high, it also self seeds very easily. Good soil is required and seeds should be planted in late spring. Cut back often for best results. Burnet leaves are a delightful change as a source of greens.

Comfrey

This wonderful perennial plant has so many uses (see medicinal section). If you have room in the garden you will really appreciate its virtues. Comfrey grows in almost any type of soil, but thrives on moist conditions. Seeds should be planted in early springtime, and later thinned to approximately 15 inches apart. Comfrey usually grows up to 3 ft. tall. The leaves are large and feel very coarse and can be added to salads or cooked like spinach. The blue or purple flowers usually bloom in May, June and July. Because of the large roots it is better to leave this plant free to grow rather than cultivate in a container.

Dandelion

Yes, I really did say dandelion! Just think you don't even have to cultivate these — they grow all over the lawn anyway. Maybe you could keep a small portion of your lawn for this valuable plant. The roots of the dandelion have many uses and should be gathered when the plant is blooming. In the springtime the young leaves can be added to salads if desired but the roots contain most of the vitamins and minerals. You can even make a delicious coffee substitute with them. Many people from Europe know the value of the dandelion as this plant originated there. See Chapter on Selected Herbs.

Dill

This is a popular herb in country areas since many people use it for flavouring pickles of all kinds. It is used medicinally for digestive disorders and has a calming effect on the system. Babies particularly benefit from a water made from the seeds. It eliminates hiccoughs and settles the tummy. It works for adults the same way. To grow dill in the garden, place the seeds in a sunny spot but remember it grows 2 to 3 feet high and does not transplant well — it is better to leave it where originally planted. Plant in early springtime. Dill gives much color to the garden and also has a delightful fragrance. Its culinary uses are many and varied, fish, salads, vegetables, soups and dips all taste wonderful with a touch of dill.

Garlic

After all the wonderful stories told about garlic it would be a shame not to include it in your herb garden. It is a perennial and likes to be in a sunny spot with moist soil. Obtain a bulb and take out the cloves, place them in the soil 2 inches deep and 6 inches apart. Check soil for moisture often. By late summer you can take out the garlic and continue to dry out for use all winter long. Since garlic contains a pungent oil it should be used sparingly in cooking — experiment until you find exactly the right amount to add. It is very versatile as a culinary plant — meats, vegetables, salads and soups are all enhanced with a touch of garlic.

Lemon Balm

This is a delightful fragrant plant this is ideal for a (deep) window box. Since the seeds take so long to germinate, it is probably easier to start with cuttings, planted 10 inches apart. They grow very quickly and need to be cut back often. The plants usually grow 1 to 2 feet high. The leaves, either dried or fresh, can be used to make the most delicious tea. I used to gather the leaves and dry them in a brown paper bag then store them in dark airtight containers for use all winter long. It truly is a refreshing taste especially if a little honey is added to the tea. For anyone wishing to be rid of the coffee or tea habit — lemon balm in a wonderful replacement. It is ideal for any dishes that require an added fruit lift (fruit compote, punch, etc). If you plan to grow it, plant enough to give your friends a cutting (they'll be friends for life).

Nasturtium

A beautiful annual plant that adds much color and charm to your garden, it is also very valuable from a medicinal point of view. Most herbalists consider this plant a natural antibiotic since it contains so many infection fighting nutrients (it is especially high in Vitamin C). The leaves or flowers can be added fresh to salads or dried if desired. Fresh leaves added to sandwiches make a welcome and delicious change from lettuce or sprouts. Nasturtiums thrive in light sandy soil and should be planted from seed, in late spring in a sunny spot.

Parsley

This is a hardy biennial but most people plant new each year. Seeds should be sown in spring, preferably where they are to stay since they do not produce well when transplanted. They thrive in lightly fertilized soil and a sunny position. Plants should be thinned to approximately 6 inches apart. Some varieties grow up to 2 feet in height. Parsley is highly nutritious and contains high amounts of vitamins and minerals (see vitamin section). It keeps well if dried and put into dark, airtight containers. I have a friend who told me she puts some into plastic bags and freezes for future use — I have never tried this myself but I certainly intend to. A valuable plant worth your time and effort in terms of good health.

Peppermint

Peppermint is a perennial that needs careful handling since it can, and often does take over a garden. It grows best in moist soil (shade or sun) and can reach a height of 2 to 3 ft. Since it spreads so quickly it is perhaps a good idea to plant it near a wall or something that will keep it apart from your other plants. Never let it go to seed or you will have a messy garden indeed. In springtime plant roots 2 inches deep and 8 inches apart. If cultivating peppermint sounds a little discouraging I can assure you it is worth the effort. Salads, soups, fruits, vegetables and teas, all benefit from peppermint's fresh flavor. It can also be chewed as a breath freshener — look at the money you can save on mouth wash.

Rosemary

Rosemary is an evergreen perennial that can grow from 15 inches to 6 feet high depending on the variety. The easiest way to grow it is from cuttings, as the seed process takes too long. Ideal soil conditions for Rosemary are dry and sandy with good sun exposure. In August take 6 inch cuttings and plant 3/4 of their length into the ground. This herb has a sweet smell and adds much as a culinary delight. It also has much to offer medicinally and from a beauty point of view (great for dark hair). (See beauty section).

Sage

This strong flavoured evergreen perennial grows approximately 12 - 16 inches high. It requires a sunny spot and thrives in any kind of soil. Plant the seeds or cuttings in springtime — plants should be at least 10 inches apart. A valuable plant to have around — great for flavouring meats, poultry, salads, soups, as well as a good medicine and beauty aid. (See sections).

INDOOR GARDENS

Many people love to grow herbs indoors and as long as suitable conditions are supplied, an indoor herb garden can be very successful. Most herbs that grow in pots outside will also grow indoors. It is very soothing to see greenery indoors, not only does it provide beauty, but it also adds oxygen to the air. Whenever I visit anyone for the first time, I never remember the furnishings but always appreciate their plants — they actually make a house a home as well as provide nutrition to your diet.

Tips To Follow

Plants need a certain amount of light so if possible put your pots near a good source. Rotate them around so that all sides of the plant are exposed at some time or other during the day. be careful if there is direct sun as they can dry out very quickly. When watering plants keep in mind the different needs of each one (don't just water everything once a week and leave it at that). Do not under-or over-water or the plants will die. Always provide proper drainage.

Plant Food

The soil of plants grown inside needs to be changed yearly, and plant food is usually needed to increase the quality of the soil. For advice on the right kind of food, phone your local nursery.

Allowing For Growth

Keep your eyes on the plants to make sure they do not get rootbound. As soon as they require a bigger pot, use new soil for the transplant.

Gathering And Preserving Herbs

Now that you have a plentiful supply of herbs growing, you need to know how and when to gather and preserve some for future use. Some culinary herbs in the home are good all year long for fresh picking, that is the best way from a nutritional standpoint. Other herbs that grow outside can be gathered at the correct time and dried (some even freeze well). Obviously the right time to pick your herbs depends on the plant. If you intend to use them fresh as you go along, pinch off the flower buds as soon as they blossom. The general rule to follow if you plan to preserve the herb is to make sure there is no moisture as this destroys flavor. The time to pick herbs for storage is when the essential oils are at their peak (just before the herb begins to flower). Pick your herbs for drying first thing in the morning after the dew has evaporated and before the heat of the sun dries them. Once you have your herbs, spray the dirt off **very lightly** with water and shake very gently. Now you are ready to preserve them — there are several ways to do this.

Hanging Method

The oldest method I'm sure is the way grandma did it. Gather the herbs in small bundles — tie the stems with string and turn them upside down with a brown paper bag tied at the neck. This is a good way of keeping the herbs dust-free and by shaking gently on the herbs (after they are dried) the bag collects them with no mess. Then they can be transferred to a dark airtight container. The best place to hang the bags is in a well ventilated area with even temperature. During grandma's time it wasn't unusual to see the bundles of herbs hung in the kitchen (with no bag). The air used to be scented with sweet smells — the only problem with this was dust accumulation on the plants. Plants dried in the bags usually take a month or more until they are ready for use.

Screens

Take a window screen (the type used in Summer) and spread out fresh leaves from the various herbs on the mesh and place in an area where they can dry undisturbed. Rotate them so that air reaches each part of the leaf for even drying (not in direct sun though). The drying time depends on the temperature. Roots and bark take longer to dry and since they have a tough exterior can be dried in the sun.

Oven

Many people dry herbs in the oven, care has to be taken not to burn the leaves though. Spread the leaves out on heavy brown paper and leave the oven door open to allow moisture to escape — keep temperature at 150 degrees and be sure to rotate the paper so that the drying is even. It may take 4 or 5 hours for the leaves to dry — they should be very brittle but still green. Seal in jars as soon as possible. If moisture gets into them after drying they have a tendency to mold.

Freezing

Since freezers became popular people took advantage of them and tried freezing many different foods. Certain of the herbs were found to react well to this method. Gather the same way and put them into small freezer bags. Make sure they are marked clearly for easy identification. After awhile you will know which herbs you use more often, then you can make your individual storing bags according to needs. Many of them could be chopped before freezing if desired.

Once you have used herbs from your own garden, I'm sure you will find the supermarket brands somewhat tasteless. Never purchase herbs in see through jars — they lose flavor as well as medicinal value, and you have no idea how old they are. You can store dried herbs (in good condition) up to 18 months. Did you know that vegetables such as celery, mustard greens, onions, spinach, peppers and watercress can be dried and powdered and used to make delicious broths all winter long? Fruits can be dried the same way, this is a wonderful treat to give a child — dried apricots, peaches, apples, pears and prunes certainly are better nutritionally than the junk synthetic sweets on the market.

Notes:

COOKING WITH HERBS

Good chefs know the value of herbs in food preparation — they can change a dish from ordinary to extraordinary. There is something exciting about being creative and original in the kitchen. It is important, however, to flavor food with herbs, not saturate them. Leaves can be crushed in the hands but seeds need a grinder. When buying herbs for culinary purposes buy them from a herb shop that stores them in dark containers and has a quick turnover. The following chart is a general indication of which herbs to use with certain foods — however experiment yourself with different ones — you may come up with a masterpiece!

Allspice	Pot roast, stews, pickles.
Anise Seed	Cakes, cookies, candy, breads, rolls.
Balm	Teas, fruit drinks, fruit salads.
Basil	Tomato dishes, soups, salads, fish, chicken, cheese dishes.
Bay leaves	Meat, poultry, soups, stews, sauces.
Caraway Seed	Bread, cookies, cakes, cheeses, salads, vegetables.
Cardamon	Breads, pastries, pickles, salads.
Cayenne	Meats, soups, egg dishes.
Celery Seed	Soups, stews, poultry, salads, pickles.
Chives	Salads, potatoes, sauces, vegetables.
Cinnamon	Baked goods, cereals, fruits, fruit juices.
Cloves	Stewed fruits, cakes, meats, fruit punches.
Coriander Seeds	Breads, cookies, cakes, meat, poultry, salads.
Cummin Seeds	Chili, Curry, sauces, salads, dressings.
Dill	Pickles, salads, vegetables, poultry, fish.
Fennel Seed	Cookies, bread, jellies, candies, salads, soups.
Garlic	Salads, meats, poultry, fish, dressings.
Ginger	Candies, baked goods, sauces, roasts, fruit drinks.
Mace	Fish, meats, gravies.
Marjoram	Meats, salads, soups, vegetables.
Mint	Lamb, vegetables, salads, fruits, fruit drinks, potatoes.
Nutmeg	Custards, puddings, cakes, stewed fruit.
Oregano	Sauces, soups, chili, stuffings.
Paprika	Vegetables, soups, poultry, meat, fish.
Parsley	Salads, soups. vegetables, garnish, fish.
Poppy Seeds	Cookies, cakes, breads, fruit salads.
Rosemary	Meat, fish, vegetables, soups, salads.
Saffron	Baked goods, fish, poultry, meats.
Sage	Poultry, fish, meats, stuffings.
Summer Savory	Fish, soups, vegetables, meats.
Tarragon	Salad dressings, fish, meat, poultry.
Thyme	Stuffings, meats, poultry, fish, egg dishes.
Turmeric	Curry, pickles, salad dressings.

Sprouts

Sprouting seeds increases their vitamin and mineral content considerably. There is no other food that can produce nutrients so quickly and without the use of chemical fertilizers. Sprouts are easy to grow (even young children can do it), and delicious and nutritious to eat. They are food that anyone can grow even without a garden. All you need is wide mouth mason jars covered at the opening with cheesecloth held on with elastic bands, a pair of dark socks and several kinds of seeds. There is a good variety of seeds and grains to sprout, alfalfa, mung beans, garbanzo, soybeans, lentils, millet, fenugreek, sunflower, mustard, cress, flax, and wheat, to name just a few. All of these are relatively inexpensive as a food source, but buy just a small quantity of each at first to see which ones you like the best.

Basic Method

First of all when buying your seeds ask for untreated (chemical free) ones. Sort through and discard any broken or dried out seeds. Rinse your seeds thoroughly and put into your jar for soaking overnight. Obviously seeds swell so the following guide gives you the approximate amounts to soak. I soak all of the seeds I use overnight with the exception of flax and chia, these two produce a mucilage when soaked so it is unnecessary to do so. Rinse seeds 2 - 3 times daily. Place a dark sock around the jar to seal out light for 2 or 3 days, then proceed as below.

Alfalfa Use 1½ Tbsps. seeds to a 1 quart jar and leave in the dark 2 to 3 days, or until sprouts are about 2" long. Then put the jar into the sun to allow the sprouts to develop the green chlorophyll. Add sprouts to sandwiches, salads, omelets, soups, etc. Very delicious!

Mung Beans

These are very delicious just by themselves, especially if they are cold and crispy — certainly good as a snack food. Put 3 tbsp. sorted beans to soak overnight. The next morning drain liquid (keep for soup), then put seeds into a mason jar. During the day rinse seeds thoroughly and drain off through cheesecloth and put jar in the dark. Three times a day is adequate rinsing, but remember to drain well. Usually 3 days is enough to produce a sweet sprout 2" - 3" long. Mung beans can be used in the same way as alfalfa but can also be used in oriental cooking. Mung beans are very popular because there is rarely a problem with souring.

Fenugreek Seeds

These seeds when sprouted have a very unusual taste — they give a lift to a salad. Anyone tasting them for the first time may not be as enthusiastic about fenugreek as mung or alfalfa, but they are really quite delicious. When these seeds soak first overnight, they need very little rinsing (in fact spraying them with water gently is actually better). Three days should produce a good sprout.

Lentils

These are extremely high quality food, especially good for vegetarians. To sprout put ⅓ cup lentils to 1 quart jar (these swell). Rinse 3 times daily, usually the sprouting time is 3 days. Can be added to salads, soups, casseroles and bread.

Soybeans

Many people become discouraged when trying to sprout soybeans. They sour if not handled properly and then taste awful. Sort through and discard poor, discolored or dried beans. Soak overnight and next morning (18 hours), then proceed the same way as other sprouts. Be sure when rinsing to thoroughly drain — too much moisture left in the jar increases chances of mold. Use ½ cup beans to 1 quart jar. Sometimes these take a little longer than 3 days and the sprouts are not very long. **Never** eat soybean sprouts raw as they contain a harmful enzyme. They can be steamed for 5 minutes or sautéed lightly in a little oil.

Other Sprouts To Try

Whole grains — rye, oats, corn, wheat, chick peas, millet, peas, beans and sunflower seeds — the list is extensive. Each member of the family can sprout something different — you will soon determine likes and dislikes. Use your imagination when preparing dishes for any meal — remember as you add sprouts you are actually adding vitamins and minerals.

Notes:

SELECTED HERBS TO KEEP YOU HEALTHY

While I was writing this book on herbs, my most difficult decision was which herbs to write about — there are so many. I have tried to choose herbs which can be used for a variety of purposes. This means that your collection of medicinal plants can be kept to a minimum. Keeping this in mind you may be surprised to see that a favourite herb of yours is not in the book — it is a matter of space, not preference.

The effects of the following herbs are explained thoroughly in section on Definitions of medicinal properties.

Agrimony

(Agrimonia Cupatoria)
Other Names: Cockleburr, Sticklewort.
Action: mild astringent, alterative, diuretic, tonic.
Parts used: Leaves, root, herb.

Agrimony grows extensively throughout North America. It can be found in woods and the edges of fields. It has long been used by the Indian for a variety of problems. It can be used externally for sores and blemishes as well as internally for the following: —

Bowel complaints,
General debility,
Bed-wetting,
Gallstones
Rheumatism,
Blood cleanser
Skin conditions
Gargle for sore throat,
Expelling worms,
Mouthwash,
Preparation — Infusion or decoction.

Alfalfa

(Medicago sativa)

Other names: Buffalo herb, lucerne.

Action: Diuretic, nutrient, tonic.

Parts used: Leaves.

Alfalfa is a deep rooted perennial plant generally recognized as a super food for animals as well as people. It has a history of medicinal use going back to 500 B.C. It is also an excellent source of nutrients and should be used freely in salads. Pregnant women benefit when a mild tea of alfalfa is taken as it helps to insure a good supply of milk for breast-feeding. Many people use alfalfa sprouts to replace extensive greens in the wintertime. From an economical standpoint, it is worthwhile teaching your young children to sprout their own supply — they love it and are apt to eat what they have grown themselves. It is valuable to use in soups as well as salads and as a beverage is certainly healthier than tea or coffee. Its nutritive properties include: —

Potassium,	Vitamin A
Calcium,	Vitamin B-12
Magnesium,	Vitamin C
Phosphorous,	Vitamin D
Iron,	Vitamin E,
	Vitamin K

Alfalfa taken as a daily beverage improves appetite, acts as a diuretic, regulates bowels and is an all round general tonic for producing a healthy body.

Aloe

(Aloe Vera)

Action: Tonic, purgative, anthelmintic.

Parts used: Juice from the leaves.

Uses: Burns, cuts, scratches, stings, eczema, athlete's foot, insect bites — in fact many skin irritations benefit from aloe vera where other remedies fail. Grown in warm climates such as Florida, Arizona, Texas and Africa, this plant is credited by many Indian Tribes as being a miracle plant because it has the ability to heal so many things. There has been much publicity given to this plant in recent years because of exaggerated claims made for it. It certainly does wonders externally! I'm sure many of you suffering from sunburn would agree to the merits of aloe. I once fell asleep on the beach in Hawaii and woke with a terrible burn, a local man offered to help by applying the juice of this plant. I couldn't believe how quickly the pain left. Used internally as a laxative and bowel conditioner it is beneficial in moderation. If you have medical complications do not use without first consulting your physician. Aloe Vera plants make a decorative addition to your home.

sparagus

(Asparagus officinalie)

Action: Diuretic, laxative, sedative.

Asparagus is a common garden vegetable that is most valuable as a medicinal aid. If taken as a tea, it is particularly good for stones in the kidneys or bladder. Taken as a decoction its effects as a diuretic are remarkable. Water in which asparagus has been cooked is good for rheumatism and gout. The tender young shoots are delicious when steamed and contain valuable vitamins and minerals. Two ounces of plant to one pint of water is an adequate amount.

Arnica

(Arnica Montana)
Common names: Leopard's bane, arnica Flowers.
Action: Diaphoretic, diuretic, emollient, expectorant, stimulant.
Parts used: Flowers, roots.
Found in North Western United States, mountain areas of Canada.
Uses: It is used externally with good results for bruises, strains, aching muscles, rheumatism. Arnica is used mainly for external use. Make a tea with a handful of flowers or roots to 16 oz. boiling water. Wring out a cloth in the tea and apply to bruises or strains. For rheumatism and painful joints, mix equal parts of fluid extract of arnica and equal amounts of witch-hazel, apply hot. It is very useful to have in the home where there are older poeple, particularly as a relief from aches and pains. Caution is advised in application, though as like the mustard plaster, blistering can result if solution is not diluted before applying.

B

Balm

(Melissa Officinalis)
Common Names: Lemon balm, sweet balm, Melissa
Action: Antispasmodic, diapharetic, stomachic.
Parts used: Whole herb, leaves.
Balm is a member of the mint family and is extremely popular as a culinary herb in North America. It has a delightful fragrance — lemon and mint combined. It is a joy to have in the garden. Its uses are not restricted to cooking, it has been used with success for colds, colic, dyspepsia, headaches and nervousness. Externally the leaves can be used for a poultice for insect bites. Make an infusion of 1 tsp. to 8 oz. boiling water and drink warm. With a little honey added it makes a very pleasant beverage to replace regular tea or coffee.

Basil

(Ocimum basilicum)
Common Names: St. John's Wort, Sweet basil.
Action: Carminative, stomachic, tonic.
Parts used: whole herb.
Originally a native of India, this plant is popular everywhere as a kitchen herb. Certainly no tomato dish is complete without it. It does, however, have much to offer from a medicinal point of view and also can be used to make potpourris and perfume. Make an infusion and drink 4 oz. twice daily for stomach cramps, vomiting, nausea and headaches.

Bladder-wrack

(Focus vesiculosis)
Common Names: fucus, black tang, cudweed.
Action: Alterative, demulcent, cutitoxic, nutrient.
Parts used: dried root, stem, leaves.
This valuable plant grows on rocks in the North Atlantic ocean. It is extremely high in nutrient salts needed by the human body to maintain good health. Charcoal obtained by burning fucus has been used since the 1700's to treat goitre and other related swellings. It is also successful as a weight loss agent if taken correctly Prepare a decoction of 2 oz. cut bladderwrack to 16 oz. distrilled water — keep covered and boil slowly for 10 minutes. Strain and cool, then put into dark bottle. Dose is 2 oz. 3 times daily between meals. Sweeten with a little honey for taste (if allowed sweetening), if not lemon juice will make it a little more palatable. Other conditions helped by fucus are rheumatism, gout and high blood pressure. People who live in areas where Bladderwrack is available, gather it and use it for many other conditions too numerous to mention. One claim that is consistent is the abundant energy experienced by people who take it on a regular basis.

Boneset

(Eupatarium perfeliatum)

Common Name: Crosswort, feverwort.

Action: Cathartic, diaphoretic tonic.

Parts used: whole herb.

This herb was used by the native Indian as a remedy for colds, fevers, rheumatism and influenza. To break a cold or the flu, make boneset into a decoction by boiling 2 oz. herb to 1 quart of water. Take half a cup twice daily (warm). This induces sweating and causes a cleansing of the stomach. Once the sweating has occurred, boneset can be taken as a cold tea. This acts as a tonic and speeds up recovery. To prepare tea as tonic use 2 oz. plant to 16 oz. boiling water (do not boil), let cool and take 1 oz. twice daily.

Borage

(Borage officinalis)

Common Names: Bugless, burrage.

Action: Demulcent, diuretic, diaphoretic.

Part Used: Herb, flowers.

This beautiful plant is a native of Europe and North America. The young tender leaves can be used in salads and are a rich source of potassium. Borage can be made into an infusion (1 tsp. to 6 oz. water), and sipped throughout the day. Externally borage is good for skin sores, itching and inflammations of all kinds. Internally it is useful in reducing fevers, stimulating the flow of mother's milk and soothing ulcers of the mouth and throat.

Buchu

(Barosma betulina)
Common Names: Short buchu.
Action: Carminative, diaphoretic, diuretic.
Part used: Leaves.
Buchu grows mostly in South Africa. It has been credited with being one of the best remedies for urinary disorders. It is mild and soothing. Make an infusion with 1 oz. of leaves to 16 oz. boiling water, steep and strain. Take 1 oz. every few hours. Scanty or painful urination, bladder and kidney inflamation are helped by the use of buchu.

Burdock

(Arctium lappa)
Common Names: Burr Seed, grass burdock
Action: Alterative, aperient, diaphoretic, diuretic.
Parts used: Leaves, roots, seeds.
Burdock is found in Europe and North America. It grows by the roadside and in waste places. All parts of the burdock are used for different purposes.
The seeds may be powdered and taken in a dosage of ½ tsp. as a diuretic. The rest may be made into a decoction (4 oz. root to 1 quart of water), and 4 oz. of this maybe taken twice a day to help rheumatism and gout. A decoction may be made from the leaves and applied externally to relieve acne or sores.

Caraway

(Carum carvi)

Action: Appetizer, carminative, stomachic

Although caraway is found wild in the Northwestern United States, we generally associate it with cultivation in our own gardens. Very popular as flavoring in cakes and confectionery, sometimes the medicinal benefits of these seeds are overlooked. Taken in hot milk they relieve colic in infants and made into a poultice for external use help bruises caused by blows or falls. The main uses though, are for griping and fermentation in the stomach due to indigestion.

Dosage — make tea by adding 2 tsp. seeds to 16 oz. boiling water — do not boil, drink freely.

Catnip

(Nepeta cateria)

Common Names: Catmint, catnip.

Action: Antispasmodic, carminative, diaphoretic.

Catnip is said to have originated in Europe and is a popular herb in North America (especially with cats). It is a member of the mint family and if you plan to grow it in your own garden be aware that it takes over very quickly. You need lots of space for this herb. Medicinally it is a good remedy for colds as it promotes sweating. Use 1 oz. herb to 16 oz. water — give warm and freely to adults — babies ¼ tsp. only. Other conditions helped are nervous headaches, insomnia, irritability, flatulence and spasms. Taken with a little honey makes it a tasty beverage.

Cayenne Pepper

(Capsicum minimum)
Common Names: Africa pepper, bird pepper, capsicum.
Action: Digestive, stimulant, tonic, irritant.
Part used: Fruit.
Cayenne is a popular herb in the kitchen because it gives a real zing to dishes such as chili or other hot sauces. It promotes warmth to the system and increased circulation and so is excellent in dishes served after skiing. Medicinally it is a general stimulant, aids digestion and stomach cramps, stimulates appetite and at the onset of a cold helps in a preventative way. Some people should use it with caution. however, All pepper is irritating and although cayenne is different than black pepper in its action, it can sometimes cause bowel irritation. If used externally for rheumatism, care should be taken not to create blisters. If reactions occur discontinue use. Take it with food to help relieve the burning sensation which occurs when cayenne is swallowed on an empty stomach.

Celery

(Apium graveolens)
Common Name: Garden celery.
Action: Aromatic, diuretic, carminative, sedative.
Part used: Leaves, root, seed.
Widely cultivated in Europe and North America as a common garden plant, this herb is extremely valuable as a medicine. Celery is considered a food for the nerves. It helps to promote a restful sleep and it is certainly healthier and less expensive than commercial aids. A tea made from the seeds helps stomach ulcers because of its anti-acid effect. Celery juice mixed with equal amounts of distilled water helps to dissolve cal-

cium deposits in the body. Celery is also beneficial for bronchitis, obesity, menstrual irregularities, retention of urine and flatulence.

hamomile

(Anthemis nobilis)
Common Names: Roman chamomile.
Action: Antispasmodic, carminative, stomachic, diaphoretic, sedative.
Parts used: Flowers, whole herb.
This wonderful herb is a longtime favourite, especially in England and Germany. Chamomile has a delightful fragrance and the daisylike flowers are an attractive addition to any garden. Chamomile has many uses as a medicine and is widely used in North America for nervous conditions, insomnia, stomach cramps, digestion, colic, nausea and vomiting, and to increase appetite. Externally it is excellent as a wash for sores and wounds, skin eruptions and as a rinse for blond hair.
Make a simple infusion with 1 tsp. flowers to 8 oz. water and sip in small amounts throughout the day. Taken an hour before bedtime it produces a restful sleep. If given for babies' colic, make a tea with 1 oz. flowers to one pint of water — give 3 or 4 teaspoons daily as needed.

Coltsfoot

(Tussilage farfara)

Common Names: Bullsfeet, coughoart, horsehoof.

Action: Demulcent, emollient, expectorant.

Parts used: Flowers, leaves.

Found in Europe as well as North America coltsfoot is noted for its effectiveness in respiratory ailments such as asthma, bronchitis, coughs, colds, congestion, hoarseness, and other pulmonary conditions. The dried leaves can be smoked for deep seated chest complaints. Externally a poultice can be applied to burns, ulcers and inflammatiions. Make an infusion of 1 tsp. leaves to 8 oz. boiling water. Steep and sip throughout the day, to help congestion and relieve a cough. Externally, make a decoction and apply directly or crush the leaves and use as a poultice.

Comfrey

(officinale)

Common Names: Blackwort, gum plant, healing herb, knitbone.

Action: Mucilaginous, expectorant, emollient.

Parts used: — Roots, leaves.

Many families grow comfrey in the garden for use in salads as well as a medicine. It is an old favourite from the middle ages and still revered today. The word officinale means it was a recognized medicine in the pharmacopoeia used by the monks in England. Comfrey is a rich source of vitamin A, B-1, B-12, and is abundant in calcium, potassium, and trace minerals. The main ingredient is allantoin, a natural cell proliferant. If a poultice is made of fresh leaves and applied to a wound, it will heal faster. Vets have discovered the usefulness of this plant in the healing of animals. Because of the high calcium content, broken bones knit together faster if comfrey tea is taken on a regular basis.

Fresh roots can be used to make a poultice and applied externally for bruises, burns, wounds, insect bites, sore breasts, ulcers. It also helps to relieve pain from gout and rheumatism.

A decoction of 1 oz. root to a quart of water is good for soreness of bowels caused by diarrhea. Chronic coughs and chest congestion are eased by drinking freely during the day. Other conditions helped by comfrey are arthritis, asthma, dysentery, leucorrhoea, internal bleeding, pleurisy, bronchitis, and general weakness of the body. Used as a gargle it eases a sore throat.

Cornsilk

(Maida stigmata)

Common Names: Indian corn, maize.

Many people do not realize the benefits of this old Indian remedy. Cornsilk is a great aid for urinary problems of all kinds such as uric acid retention, cystitis, kidney and bladder disorders and it is especially good for bed-wetting problems in children. Make a tea and have one cup 3 times daily before meals. A tea made of 1 tsp. powdered cornsilk will help relieve nausea and vomiting.

Dandelion

(Taraxacum officinale)

Common Names: Blowball, lions tooth, wild endive.

Action: Diaphoretic, diuretic, expectorant, tonic, alterative.

Parts used; Flowers, leaves, root.

A longtime favourite of herbalists everywhere, dandelion grows on your front lawn with no problem. Though people curse it because it is so hardy, the dandelion has surprising value as a medicine and a food. The roots should be gathered in the fall and are excellent used as a laxative and a tonic for the liver and the gallbladder. The flowers and leaves can be used as a tonic to tone up the whole system, especially in the spring. The vitamin and mineral content of dandelion is very high, especially in vitamins A and C and calcium and magnesium. It would be a good idea to include dandelion greens in your salad as a source of nutrients. The juice of the stems has been used for warts with good success. Combined with yellow dock it works well as a blood purifier.

Make an infusion of 1 oz. dried flowers to 16 oz. water — drink several glasses daily. This is a tonic for the whole system — and has value in treatment of billious attacks, neuralgia, skin problems (eczema), digestion, gout and retention of urine. Add a little honey to sweeten the drink.

Echinacea

(Echinacea-angustifolia)

Common Names: Black sampson, caneflower.
Action: Alterative, antiseptic, diaphoretic.
Parts used: Root.

Herbalists have long regarded echinacea as a natural antitoxin. It was used by the Sioux Indians for blood poisoning, snake bites, etc. Externally applied, it seems to help conditions such as boils, carbuncles, sores, wounds, ulcers, bites and stings. Internally it has an ability to build up the body defences and help to resist infection. Orthodox medicine does not recognize this plant as a replacement for antibiotics. Native people, however, regarded echinacea as one of the most useful plants for prevention of all blood infections.

Internally: Prepare a decoction — 1 tsp. Root to 8 oz. water. Take 1 Tbsp. 3 times daily.

Externally: Prepare as above — apply to affected parts.

Note: Do not use root after the odour is lost. Tinctures of this herb can be purchased at herb stores everywhere. We keep one in our medicine chest ready to use if necessary.

Elder

(Sambucus Canadensis)

Common Names: Blackberried elder, sweet elder, elder flowers.

Action: Alterative, diuretic, diaphoretic, expectorant, emetic, purgative.

Parts used: Inner bark, berries, flowers.

Elder is a popular herb used by many cultures throughout the world for a variety of uses. It grows extensively in Canada and the United States. It is probably familiar to you as delicious elderberry wine, and you may have enjoyed elderberry jelly and pies.

A tea made from the flowers greatly promotes sweating so at the onset of a cold or flu it helps eliminate toxins from the body. A mixture of half peppermint leaves and half elder leaves is even better. The root made into tea and taken internally is said by the Indians to help promote labour in childbirth. It also takes fluid out of the system. No part of the elder should be eaten raw — vomiting and diarrhea can occur. An ounce of elder flowers to 16 oz. boiling water makes a good tea that helps to bring out the eruption of measles.

Externally: The flowers of elder contain an essential oil that is used in the making of cosmetics. It is known for its beneficial effects on the skin. Eye problems can be helped by bathing in cool Elder flower water.

F

Fennel

(Faeniculum uulgare)
Common Names: Sweet Fennel, Wild Fennel.
Action: Aromatic, carminative, expectorant, stomachic.
Parts used: Seeds, leaves.
Found extensively in Europe, this herb is also widely cultivated in North America. When the seeds are crushed, a strong anise-like fragrance exudes that is delightful to smell. It is excellent for all digestive problems, dyspepsia and colic in particular, stimulates appetite and is most effective as a gargle for hoarse throat. To make a tea, use 1 oz. seed to 16 oz. water, take 1 tsp. 3 times daily (good for stimualting flow of mother's milk). For culinary purposes, breads and cookies taste better for the addition of fennel.
Externally: it has been known to help insect stings.

Fenugreek

(Trigonella foenum graecum)
Action: expectorant, mucilaginous, restorative.
Widely used in North America for medicine and culinary purposes, fenugreek is an old and trusted herb used by the ancient Egyptians. Sprouted it makes a good addition to salads and gives a good flavor. Make a decoction of 2 tsp. of these seeds to 8 oz. cold water. Bring to boil for one minute, and drink 2 cups daily. Taken in this manner fenugreek is good for relieving flatulence and upset stomach. It is also very beneficial for sinus conditions and allergy sufferers. It relieves congestion in the bronchials and as a gargle for sore throat is one of the most effective herbs there is.
Externally: a poultice can be used for external use in the healing of skin infections, sores and wounds.

Garlic

(Allium sativum)

Common Names: Poor man's treacle.

Action: Antiseptic, digestive, diuretic, expectorant, febrifuge.

Part used: Bulb.

Garlic is used throughout the world for culinary and medicinal purposes. So much has been written about this wonderful herb — everyone, it seems, has a story to tell of its miraculous healing powers. In Japan there is an institute of healing that has several therapies where garlic is used exclusively, one of which is a cabinet designed so that the body is saturated with garlic steam to purge impurities from the system. Since garlic is high in sulphur it has a pungent smell that some people find objectionable. It also stays in the system after consumption, but the benefits far outweigh the objections. There are several ways to prepare garlic. For tea, press a garlic clove into a cup, add hot water and drink. This is especially good at the beginning of the flu or a severe cold. Chew fresh parsley after to help the odour. Taken as a tincture, cold extract, or eaten raw with a little honey garlic is most beneficial. If garlic is preserved with alcohol it will keep for several months. Conditions such as coughs, colds, bronchitis, croup, intestinal complaints, sinus conditions, digestive disorders and fevers are all helped with garlic. Whenever a poultice is made, be sure to use with olive oil to prevent burning the skin. Some people complain that garlic causes stomach upset, flatulence and headaches but this is an indication that too much is being used. Cut down quantity and remember this plant is very potent as well as valuable. Children particularly need very minute amounts.

Ginger

(Zingiber officinale)

Common Names African ginger, race ginger.

Action: Carminative, condiment, diaphoretic, stimulant.

Part used Root.

Ginger is an excellent herb to keep in the kitchen. It is useful as a remedy for colds and billious attacks as well as an excellent digestive aid. Ginger tea when taken hot causes sweating and helps to promote warmth to the body, is excellent if taken this way at the first sign of a cold. It is also valuable for menstrual cramps and upset stomach due to nerves. A tincture of ginger (1 to 4 drops every 2 hours) can be used for chronic diarrhea with good results. Chew raw for a sore throat. When making a tea use ½ tsp. to 8 oz. boiling water and add honey if desired. In cooking ginger is used for candies, cookies and sauces. I often use ginger in skim milk along with sesame tahini as a replacement for a snack during the day — very relaxing.

Ginseng

(Panaz quinquefelium)

Common Names: Redberry. five fingers.

Action: Tonic, stimulant, stomachic.

Parts used Root, leaves.

So much can be said, and has been said, about the curative effects of the wonder herb ginseng. Eastern countries particularly revere this plant and credit it with being a panacea (good for everything). Grown in America mostly for export to other countries, it is so popular that crops are sold almost before harvesting. Asiatic Ginseng is mostly cultivated in Korea and is very much the same biologically as the American species. It would not be unreasonable to assume that the American ginseng is shipped to Korea for processing and then transported back to North America for distribution at considerable cost. One thing is certain though, advocates of ginseng consider it a reasonable price to pay for its rejuvenating qualities.

During the 1920's Hollywood gave ginseng the reputation of being an aphrodisiac. The fact that it is stimulating to the nervous system and to various glands may account for an increase in the libido, thus earning it the title of the sex herb. Ginseng improves the appetite, strengthens the stomach and invigorates the entire system. Russian studies indicate that the vascular system is improved with ginseng and as a general tonic it seems to be the number one choice of the Chinese people. Since these two countries are known for their extensive studies into medicinal plants, it would seem their findings have credibility. Ginseng has been used for thousands of years and has an interesting heritage — and according to the Russians has a part to play in the future since it apparently helps to eliminate strontium 90 from the body.

Preparation — An infusion can be made from the leaves and sipped throughout the day. The powdered roots can be used by the teaspoonful as a tonic or the liquid can be purchased and taken twice daily. This herb is available in many forms, powder, leaves, liquid, capsules, tablet and granules — the choice is yours. Wild ginseng seems to be more potent than the cultivated variety. To try its effects, purchase a small amount.

Golden Seal

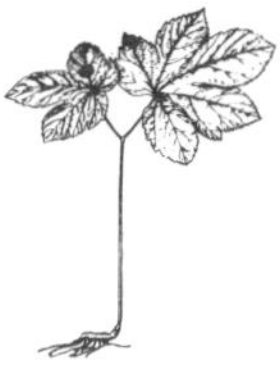

(Hydrastis canadensis)
Common Names: Yellow Puccoon, orange root, tumeric root.
Action Alterative, tonic, laxative, antiseptic.
Parts used: Root.
A native of North America and a favourite herb of the Cherokee Indian, Golden Seal has many uses both internal and external. It is extremely bitter to the taste and for that reason many people prefer to try other herbs that have similar properties. It is, however, one of the most valuable plants in the herb kingdom. An infusion can be used as a wash externally for sore inflamed eyes, skin problems such as acne, eczema, ringworm or hard to heal wounds. It is soothing to the mucous membranes so can be used as a vaginal douche as well as a gargle for sore throat. It is also very useful for dyspepsia if taken after meals.
To make an infusion use 1 tsp. powdered root to 16 oz. boiling water, let cool, use internally or externally.

Horsetail

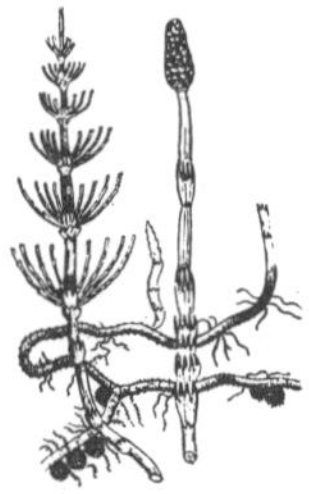

(Equisetum cruense)
Common Names: Shave Grass, horsetail
Action: Astringent, diuretic.
Part used: Plant.
American Indians and the pioneers gathered horsetail stems for use as a diuretic and also for cystitis, stomach ulcers, skin disorders, leucorrhea, liver disorders and excessive menstrual flow. Externally it is used as a wash for sores, wounds and other skin eruptions.
Preparation — to make an infusion steep 1 tsp. to 4 oz. water, drink twice daily.

Hollyhock

(Althace resea)
Common Name: Malva flowers.
Action: Demulcent, emollient.
Part used: Flowers.
Hollyhock is a beautiful plant to look at — tall, graceful with flowers that come in many colours. It is widely cultivated for its' aesthetic effect in the garden. As a medicine it can be used for inflammations of the mucous surfaces (stomach, bowels and throat). The flowers can be used to make a gargle for sore throat and it is also of benefit for pyorrhea. Drunk as a tea it is helpful for leucorrhea.
Preparation — make a simple infusion — use as needed.

Hops

(Humulus lupulus)
Action: Diuretic, tonic, nervine.
Hops have been used traditionally as a tonic during convalescence as they are helpful for a weak digestion. They are also extremely effective as a sedative and help to promote sleep. For external use, place hops in a cheesecloth moistened with hot water and apply to painful areas. Earache and toothache particularly benefit from this fomentation. To make a simple tea, use 2 tbsp. hops

to one quart of water. For nervous conditions, take 2 oz. tea three times daily. A small doses as a tonic to the system, a larger does acts as a sedative. Since so many people have to resort to sleeping pills, it would seem that a simple remedy such as hop tea would be another alternative — at very little cost.

Horehound

Common Names: White Horehound, marrubium.
Action: Diaphoretic, expectorant, tonic, laxative.
Part used: Leaves.
Many of us remember horehound as a delicious candy taken to help relieve a cough. Indeed, it is still used today in pharmacy as a vital ingredient in cough medicines. The ancient Egyptians as well as the Romans, used it so from a traditional point of view it is well established. Horehound grows along fences and roadsides all over Canada, the United States and Europe. The leaves are very wrinkled, the flowers white and the plant has a musk-like odour.
Preparation — infuse 1 tsp. leaves in 8 oz. hot water. Steep, strain, take 1 oz. at a time to a total of 2 cups daily. Add honey if desired. This can be taken for coughs, colds, and lung problems.

Horse-radish

(Cochlearia armoracia)

Action: Diuretic, stomachic, stimulant.

Horseradish is mostly associated as an accompaniment to roast beef, however, it has much to offer as a medicinal herb. A native of Europe originally, it is now popular world-wide. 1 oz. of the root to one quart water makes a tea that is valuable for rheumatism, gout, neuralgia and dropsy. For nasal problems, catarrh, coughs or asthma, take horseradish with a little honey. Externally it can be used as a poultice (like mustard), but it must not be put directly on the skin. Put inside cloth and apply against affected part until burning is felt. Remember that horseradish is a powerful stimulant and should be used with caution. Only the fresh herb should be used.

Licorice

(Glycyrrhiza glabra)
Common Name: Sweet wood
Action: Demulcent, expectorant, laxative.
Part used: Dried root.

Licorice root resembles a wrinkled tree bark with a yellow fiber inside. School children in England during the war years used this root as a substitute for candy which was unavailable. It can taste sweet or bitter depending when the roots were taken from the soil. Commercially it is used by many industries, as a flavoring agent. The list is varied: candy; beer; soft drinks; liquor; and even tobacco. Medicinally it is mainly used for bronchial problems, coughs, hoarseness, sore throat and congestion. Pharmaceutical companies use large amounts for various medicines. Singers very often use this herb to keep their throats from becoming hoarse. It has also been used in stomach problems such as peptic ulcers with soothing results. Licorice has been around for a long time and was held by the Egyptians and Chinese in high regard.

Preparation can be an infusion or decoction — use 1 tsp to 8 oz. water — dose ½ cup twice daily. The root can also be chewed (I hope it's a sweet one!).

Lungwort

(Pulmonaria officinalis)
Common Names: Spotted lungwort, jerusalem cowslip.
Action: Demulcent, expectorant, emollient.
Parts Used: Leaves.
This herb is well known to anyone who has studied folk medicine. It has the reputation of being an indispensable plant for lung problems (hence the name) both in Europe and North America. Some people cultivate it in the garden and claim it is beneficial for external use as well. From a nutritional standpoint, lungwort has been found to contain valuable vitamins and minerals, thus it is helpful in repairing and building body tissue. As a treatment for coughs, colds, asthma and bronchial inflammation, prepare an infusion of 2 oz. herb to 16 oz. boiling water — sip throughout the day, 2 oz. at a time 4 times daily. Externally it can be used to wash wounds since it is also very antiseptic.

Marigold

(Calendula officinalis)
Common Name: Pot Marigold.
Action: Astringent, stimulant, diaphoretic.
Parts Used: Leaves, flowers.
A beautiful addition to the garden, Marigolds are easy to grow and do not require any particular kind of soil. Believed to have originated in India, the Marigold has the distinction of being mentioned in a poem by Shakespeare. Apart from the aesthetic qualities, Marigold petals can be made into ointments and applied externally for cuts, burns, bruises, sprains, sore muscles and related ailments with excellent results. An in-

fusion of 2 oz. flowers and leaves to 16 oz. boiling water can be made to bathe hard-to-heal external wounds; inflamed eyes and as a wash for wasp and bee stings. Internally an infusion of 1 tsp. to 8 oz. water can be taken once a day to induce perspiration and to help bring out measles in children. It's a useful herb to have in your garden.

Marjoram

(Origanum majorana)
Common Names: Sweet marjoram, knotted marjoram.
Action: Antispasmodic, diaphoretic, stomachic, tonic.
Parts Used: Whole herb.
Marjoram is famous for its aromatic qualities and is used as a culinary herb throughout the world. Salads, poultry, soups and vegetables all taste better for the addition of Marjoram as a seasoning. Even cosmetics are scented with it. Medicinally, marjoram is beneficial as a general tonic for the whole system. It relieves vertigo and upset stomach after eating, and is used for relief of colic in children. Externally it helps bruises, varicose veins and stiff joints. To make an infusion, use 1 tsp. herb to 8 oz. boiling water, steep for 10 minutes — strain and drink. If allowed, honey may be used to sweeten. Drink 1 cup daily. To use for bruises, mix powdered herb with a little honey and apply externally.

Mullein

(Verbiscum thapsus)

Common Names: Velvet plant, shepherds club, flannel flower.

Action: Emollient, sedative, demulcent, expectorant.

Parts Used: Leaves, flowers.

When all others fail, try mullein — such is the reputation of this versatile plant. Along the roadside in North America a common sight is the tall spikey mullein so well regarded by herbalists everywhere. Invaluable for treatment of coughs, colds, lung congestion and asthma, it is probably most famous for its effectiveness in treating pulmonary complaints. It is also very helpful for other conditions externally. A fomentation of mullein leaves in vinegar and water makes a useful remedy for inflamed piles, ulcers or sore throat, and a poultice can be made for sprains and swellings. For an earache, a few warm drops of mullein is very effective.

Preparation — for bronchial conditions infuse 1 tsp. of leaves to 8 oz. boiling water — drink 2 cups daily. External use — follow directions as for fomentation and poultices on pages 82 and 83.

Nasturtium

(Trapaeolum majus)

Common Names: Indian cress.

Action: Antiseptic, expectorant.

Parts Used: Flowers, leaves, seeds.

Nasturtium is believed to have its origin in South America but is cultivated on a universal scale as an attractive addition to the garden. It is believed by many herbalists to be a natural antibiotic. The leaves and stems are used in sandwiches (rather like cress) to liven up the palate. They are also used in salads and give a spicy flavor. A tea taken internally is used to clear up infections and is helpful for chest congestion.

Nettle

(Urtica dioica)
Common Name: Stinging nettle.
Action: Astringent, diuretic, tonic.
Parts used: Roots, leaves.

Nettle is a plant common to North America and grows in waste places and along roadsides. For those who have experienced a stinging sensation after coming in contact with nettle, there is no doubt as to why the plant earned its common name. The juice of the plant will heal the irritation caused by the stinging. Tea made with nettle is helpful to clear the lungs of phlegm and to help normalize heavy menstrual flow. Diarrhea is also helped with this tea. Externally, nettle has been credited with conditioning the scalp and helping to stop hair loss. A poultice made of the leaves helps to alleviate rheumatic pain and discomfort. Since the young leaves have lots of iron and potassium they can be added to a salad as a nutritional bonus (only young leaves should be used).

The leaves are also good to stop bleeding externally — just apply bruised leaves to affected area.

Preparation — make a decoction — take 2 oz. 3 times daily for diarrhea, dysentery and piles. For scalp treatment massage into the hair after shampoo for several minutes each time you wash hair. There are several good nettle treatments from England available at natural herb shops if you prefer to use one already made up.

Onion

(Allium cepa)

Action: Antiseptic, carminative, diuretic, expectorant.

The onion is cultivated in gardens everywhere both as a food and medicine. Very high in sulphur, onions are excellent as an antiseptic and blood purifier. Unlike garlic (same family) onions are a little more versatile and can be prepared many more ways to help various problems. Raw onions kill worms and combined with honey, they make a cough syrup that is hard to beat. Onion juice for asthma and bronchitis is very effective, and at the start of a cold it acts as a preventative. When made into a poultice they are good for drawing out infections (boils) etc. and grated raw onions take the fire out of burns. The vitamin content of onions is high so to add them to a salad is certainly a plus. They also help to lower blood pressure. Taken in moderation, onions reduce flatulence, but if consumed to excess, they may actually increase that condition.

Preparation — sprinkle honey on chopped raw onions and leave overnight. This forms a syrup useful for coughs or croup. Take by the teaspoonful.

Parsley

(Petroselinum sativum)

Common Names: Rock parsley, garden parsley.

Action: Aperient, diuretic, expectorant.

Parts Used: Leaves, roots, seeds.

Parsley is another herb known worldwide for its delicious flavor in soups, salads, stews and of course as an attractive garnish. It has however much to offer from a medicinal point of view. As a preventative it is extremely good for cleansing the body. It is rich in vitamins and minerals especially calcium, magnesium and potassium. Drinking parsley tea on a regular basis helps prevent the formation of gallstones. It is beneficial for an upset stomach, painful menstruation, retention of urine, cleansing the liver, and inflammation of the bladder. To prepare a tea, use 1 oz. parsley to 16 oz. water. Dose is 2 oz. taken warm 3 times daily. Externally, parsley leaves can be used to soothe bruises, swollen glands and a fomentation can be applied to insect stings with good results. An abundance of parsley in a salad daily would be a nutritional plus — one of those herbs that is a must to grow in your garden.

Pepper-mint

(Mentha piperita)

Common Names: Brandy mint, white mint.

Action; Aromatic, carminative, stimulant, tonic.

Parts Used: Whole herb.

Believed to have originated in Europe, peppermint is now cultivated in the United States because of its value as a flavoring agent. The oil extracted from the plant contains menthol which is used in dental preparations, candy, medicines and cosmetics. Peppermint tea is invaluable as a digestive aid, and when mixed with equal amounts of elder flowers is an old favorite to relieve a cold. It is useful in the treatment of hysteria and helps to check nausea and vomiting. Babies can be given a ¼ tsp. at a time to help colic and is soothing to them when teething. Prepare an infusion by using 1 oz. herb to 1 quart boiling water. Drink as needed. Honey can be added as a sweetener if desired. Pure peppermint oil can be purchased at herb shops, 2 drops in a cup of hot water relieves indigestion very quickly.

Plantain

(Plantago major)

Common Name: Englishman's foot, ripple grass.

Action: Astringent, alterative, diuretic, demulcent.

Parts Used: Whole plant.

Plantain was a favorite with the North American Indian because of its versatility as well as its availability. It grows everywhere and is a valuable aid both internally and externally. The Chinese look upon plantain as a remedy for loss of sexual appetite and to promote fertility. It has a high concentrate of calcium and potassium and this may explain why birds seek out the seeds as food. The powdered root can be made into a tea that is useful as a douche to check leucorrhea. It is also used to prevent bed-wetting if 1 oz. is taken an hour before retiring. An infusion of the leaves can be used for diarrhea, coughs, kidney and bladder problems, ulcers, gastritis and internal bleeding. The bruised leaves can be applied externally to bites, stings, and a paste of the leaves will stop bleeding. The pain of piles can be eased by the application of fresh bruised leaves to affected area.

Preparation — Infusion 1 tsp. leaves to 4 oz. water. Take twice daily.

Externally — leaves can be bruised and applied directly or can be made into a powder and applied as a paste.

Raspberry

(Rubus idacus)

Common Name: Wild red raspberry.

Action: Astringent, stimulant, tonic.

Parts Used: Leaves, berries.

Raspberry is a member of the rose family and grows wild as well as being cultivated in gardens. It is most famous as a delicious fruit to be made into jams and jellies. Its medicinal qualities should not be overlooked. Raspberry is the pregnancy herb — it helps to strengthen the uterine muscles and makes for an easier delivery. It is also helpful for morning sickness and can be taken freely thoughout pregnancy. For anyone who has problems with miscarriages, it may be the answer — it was certainly used by the Indian women with great success. Other uses for this herb include diarrhea, regulates menstruation, mononucleosis, leucorrhea and acts as a gargle for a sore mouth and a wash for skin sores.

Infusion — prepare 1 tbs. leaves to 8 oz. water — steep and drink freely.

Red Clover

(Trifolium pratense)
Common Name: Trefoil, purple clover.
Action: Alterative, diuretic, sedative.
Parts Used: Blossoms, leaves.

Red Clover can be seen growing wild along the roadside and in fields all over North America. It is said to be an excellent blood purifier and a treatment for scrufula, bronchitis, coughs, skin diseases, sores, wounds and ulcers, anemia, athlete's foot, sore throat and vaginal irritations. Red Clover is known to herbalists as an aid in cancerous conditions. This however, is not recognized by orthodox medical circles. A tea made from the blossoms could be taken in place of regular tea and coffee with beneficial results. (use 2 oz. clover tops to 8 oz. boiling water, steep 15 minutes — 3 cups daily). For external use make a strong infusion and bathe affected parts.

Sage

(Salvia officinalis)
Common Name: Garden sage.
Action: Astringent, expectorant, stimulant, tonic.
Parts Used: Leaves.

Sage has been held in high esteem since ancient times and continues to be praised by herbalists everywhere for its medicinal properties. There are many species of sage and all are equally valuable as medicine. As a seasoning for soups and poultry dressing, sage is well known because of its strong odor. It is widely cultivated in North American gardens and the leaves can be dried and stored for all year use. An infusion of 4 oz. sage to 1 pint of boiling water can be made and taken by the tablespoon throughout the day up to 1 cup total. It is excellent for nervous complaints, headaches, colds, fevers, night sweats, worms and diarrhea. For a sore throat and laryngitis use the tea as a gargle (a little honey added helps). Externally, a decoction can be used for massaging the scalp to help dandruff and, added to bath water it relieves itchy skin.

Senna

(Cassia marilandica)
Common Name: Locust plant, wild senna
Action: Cathartic, laxative, vermifuge.
Parts Used: Leaves.
Senna is used mainly as a laxative and as such is extremely effective. It does have a tendency to cause cramping in some people. To counteract this problem, use in combination with anise, caraway or ginger. It is also used to expel worms and to prevent billiousness. It should not be used by pregnant women or by those with a hemorrhoid problem.
To prepare an infusion ½ tsp. leaves with 1 cup boiling water is usually sufficient, add a pinch of one of the above aromatic herbs, steep 15 minutes and take 2 oz. before bedtime as a laxative.

Slippery Elm

(Ulmus fulva)
Common Name: Indian Elm, American Elm.
Action: Demulcent, emollient, nutritive.
Parts Used: Inner bark dried.
Slippery Elm is soothing and nutritious and is especially helpful for anyone recuperating after an illness. Any problem involving inflammation of the mucous membrane of the stomach or bowel responds well to slippery elm. Ground into a powder and made into a poultice, it can be used externally for ulcers, wounds and boils.
Preparation for internal use — 1 tsp. bark to 8 oz. boiling water, steep 20 minutes. To make a nourishing drink to replace food, it can be made with hot milk and flavored with honey.

Straw-berry

(Fragaria vesca)

Action: Astringent, diuretic, tonic.

Strawberries are not only delicious as a dessert, but are extremely valuable for anyone suffering from kidney or bladder problems and should be eaten frequently (without sugar). A tea made from the leaves is helpful to anyone with anemia since it has an abundance of natural iron, which is easy to assimilate. Synthetic iron has a tendency to constipate so these leaves would be a good alternative if iron is needed. A strong decoction of the leaves can be used as a gargle and a treatment for spongy gums, as well as diarrhea. Externally skin erruptions heal faster after bathing with strawberry leaf tea.

Preparation — 1 oz. dried leaves to 8 oz. boiling water, steep 10 minutes — drink 3 cups daily.

Thyme

(Thymus vulgaris)

Common Name: Common thyme.

Action: Antispasmodic, carminative, diaphoretic, tonic.

Parts Used: Whole herb.

Thyme is a well cultivated herb that is famous as a flavoring agent, especially in turkey stuffing. It is valuable for headaches, dizziness, painful menstruation, flatulence, bronchitis, dyspepsia and to induce perspiration during a cold. To prepare use 2 oz. plant to 1 pint water. Take warm by the tablespoon up to 1 cup per day.

Valerian

(Valerian officinalis)
Common Name: Wild valerian, capons tail.
Action: Antispasmodic, calmative, tonic, ner vine.
Parts Used Root.

Valerian is used today by most herbalists as a sedative and usually taken along with other herbs such as skullcap, blue vervain and mistletoe. It is a very effective nerve tonic. Generally considered to be gentle in its action on the system, it can cause the opposite of the desired effect if taken too frequently, or in large doses. During the middle ages this herb was regarded as a panacea because of the variety of ailments for which it was used. Epilepsy, hysteria, insomnia, female problems, coughs, lung congestion and water retention were just a few of them. The odor of valerian is not very pleasant and for that reason many people take a prepared formula in tincture or capsule form. There are several brands available. It is very important to follow directions correctly when taking any herbal formula. To prepare an infusion of valerian, use 1 tsp. powdered root to 1 pint of boiling water, steep 5 minutes, add honey and take by the wineglass during the day as needed or before retiring, up to 1 cup daily.

Water-cress

(Nasturtina officinale)
Common Name: Scurvy grass, tall nasturtium.
Action: Diuretic, stimulant, tonic, blood purifier.
Parts Used: Leaves, roots.

Watercress can be found along moist banks of the river and in shallow river beds in most areas of North America as well as Europe. It has long been recognized as a good source of vitamins and minerals, particularly vitamin C and vitamin E. It was used by the American Indian to dissolve kidney stones. John Lust in his excellent herb book, cautions against excessive use of watercress, especially during pregnancy. Fresh watercress added to your salad once or twice weekly would probably be sufficient as a good source of nutrients. Externally, the juice of the leaves applied to skin eruptions such as pimples, sores, and eczema is very beneficial.

Yarrow

(Achillea millefelium)
Common Names: Thousand leaf, milfeil, old man's pepper
Action: Alterative astringent, diuretic, tonic.
Parts Used: The herb.
Yarrow is cultivated in gardens for use as a medicine. It also grows wild in many areas throughout the world. It can be found in fields, woods and pastures and it flowers most of the summer. It should be gathered while in bloom. Medicinally yarrow seems to be extremely useful for childhood diseases such as measles and chickenpox and is valuable in treating severe colds and fevers. It has been used for incontinence of urine, dysentery, leucorrhea and profuse menstruation. To prepare, infuse 1 tsp. to 8 oz. boiling water, take by the wineglass 3 times daily. Externally, a poultice can be used to staunch wounds. It stops bleeding effectively, thus earning it the nick-name of Staunch weed. It is one of the old beloved herbs used by the Greeks and still recommended today by herbalists everywhere.

DEFINITIONS OF MEDICINAL PROPERTIES

ALTERATIVES

A term used for substances that change body conditions usually for the better, by working on the organs of nutrition. The human system sometimes runs into problems through incorrect diet and a lack of fresh, unpolluted air.

- Alder bark
- Barberry
- Bayberry root
- Beetroot
- Bittersweet twigs
- Black cohosh root
- Blood root
- Buckbean leaves
- Burdock root
- Chickweed
- Comfrey
- Echinacea root
- False unicorn
- Figwort
- Fringe tree bark
- Golden Seal root
- Hops
- Lemon
- Oregon grape root
- Pimpernel
- Pipissiwa
- Plantain leaves
- Pokeroot
- Red clover
- Soaproot
- Squaw vine
- Yellow dock
- White oak bark

Anodyne

Used to relieve pain.

Bittersweet root,
Catnip,
Hops,
Indian hemp,
Lady's Slipper,
Mullein,
Nettle tree bark,
Passion flowers,
Peppermint.

Antibilious

Used to counteract billiousness by affecting the bile.

American centaury,
Angustara bark,
Chamomile,
Fennel,
Tumeric.

Antiemetic

Stops vomiting — relieves nausea.

Anise,
Cloves,
Columba root,
Fennel,
Horsemint,
Peach leaves,
Peppermint,
Wild red raspberry leaves.

Antilithics

Used to prevent formation of gravel and stones in urinary organs.

Buchu leaves,
Bearberry leaves,
Golden rod,
Hydrangea root,
Uva-Ursi.

Antiperiodic

Used to help prevent periodic return of chills and fevers.

Barberry,
Buckbean,
Black cohosh (root)
Boneset,
Cedron seeds,
Cramp bark,
Golden Seal (root)
Ironwood bark,
Persimmon bark,
Rosemary,
White willow bark,
Vervain leaves.

Antirheumatics

Herbs said to correct and relieve rheumatism, arthritis, sciatica, gout.

Bearsfoot root,
Birch (bark),
Black alder bark,
Black cohosh root,
Burdock,
Cayenne,
Chapparal,
Culvers root,
Elder flowers,
False bittersweet,
Horehound,
Horseradish root,
Prickly ash bark,
Skunk cabbage,
Yellow dock root.

Antiseptics

Used to prevent infections and the formation of pus.

Amaranth leaves,
Bethroot,
Black alder bark,
Blood root,
Couch grass,
Cornsilk,
Comfrey,
Cranesbill root,
Echinacea,
Golden seal,
Myrrh,
Onion,
St. Johnswort,
Wild sage leaves.

Antispasmodic

Herbs said to prevent spasms, cramps, and muscular irritability.

Bethroot,
Black cohosh root,
Cassia bark,
Catnip,
Celery seed,
Chamomile flowers,
Hops,
Linden flowers,
Mullein leaves,
Passion flower,
Rosemary,
Spikenard,
Vervain.

Aperient

Herbs used as mild, gentle laxative.

Asparagus,
Borage,
Cascara sagrada,
Dandelion root,
Flaxseed,
Marshallow,
Parsley root,
Rhubarb,
Senna,
Wood betony leaves.

Aphrodisiacs

Said to improve sexual appetite.

Betal,
Echinacea,
Damiana leaves,
Summer savory.
Ginseng

Aromatics

Substances that have a pleasant taste — often added to other herbs to make them more palatable.

Anise seeds,
Basil,
Bayberry leaves,
Calamint,
Caraway seeds,
Caraway,
Cardamom
Celery seed,
Cinnamon bark,
Cloves,
Coriander seeds,
Cumin,
Dill,
Fennel,
Garden sage,
Ginger root,
Lemon balm,
Nutmeg,
Orange peel,
Parsley,
Peppermint,
Thyme.

Astringents

Said to produce contraction of tissues and arrest discharges (e.g. from urinary tracts, uterus, etc.).

African ginger,
Blackberry root,
Buchu,
Cayenne pepper,
Cinnamon bark,
Comfrey root,
Goldenrod,
Horsemint,
Hydrangea,
Lungwort,
Nettle leaves,
Raspberry leaves,
Rosemary,
Strawberry leaves,
White ash bark,
Witch Hazel (bark and leaves),
Yarrow.

Carminatives

Expels wind from the bowels.

Anise seeds,
Caraway seeds,
Cardamom
Celery seeds,
Cinnamon,
Coriander,
Cloves,
Dill,
Fennel,
Ginger root,
Horseradish,
Lemon balm,
Nutmeg,
Parsley root,
Peppermint leaves,
Rosemary,

Cathartic

An agent used to empty the bowels. Purgative.

Aloe
Barberry,
Buckthorn,
Cascara bark,
Culver's root,
Licorice,
Mandrake,
Pansy,
Rhubarb root,
Senna leaves.

Chalagogues

Herbs which have a beneficial effect upon the liver to increase the flow of bile.

Aloe,
Barberry bark,
Blessed thistle,
Butternut,
Chicory root,
Culver's root,
Dandelion root,
False bittersweet,
Fringe tree bark,
Mandrake,
Parsley.

Condiments

Herbs used to flavor foods.

Anise,
Basil,
Bay leaves,
Caraway,
Cardamom
Cayenne,
Celery seeds,
Chives,
Cinnamon
Cloves,
Coriander seeds,
Cumin seeds,
Dill,
Fennel,
Garlic,
Ginger,
Mace,
Nutmeg,
Oregano,
Paprika,
Parsley,
Peppermint,
Poppy seed,
Rosemary,
Saffron,
Sage,
Savoury,
Tarragon,
Thyme,
White mustard seed.

Demulcents

These herbs are said to soothe and relieve inflammation. Especially beneficial to inflamed mucuous membrane of throat, lungs, stomach and intestines.

Acacia,
Chickweed,
Coltsfoot leaves,
Comfrey root,
Cornsilk,
Fenugreek,
Flaxseed,
Licorice root,
Marshmallow
Mullein (leaves and flowers),
Plantain,
Slippery elm.

Depuratives

Blood Cleansers — useful in removing waste.

Bittersweet,
Burdock root,
Chaparral,
Culver's root,
Dandelion root,
Dulse,
Elder flowers,
Linden flowers,
Meadow sweet,
Pansy,
Red clover,
Watercress,
Yellow dock root.

Detergents

Herbs used to cleanse wounds such as boils and ulcers externally.

Balm of Gilead bark,
Bloodroot,
Golden seal root,
Hyssop,
Plantain,
Red clover flowers,
Shepherd's purse,
Southern-wood,
Yellow dock.

Diaphoretic

Herbs which produce sweating.

American Pennyroyal,
Anise seed,
Bittersweet,
Black birch leaves,
Boneset,
Burdock root,
Catnip,
Cayenne,
Chamomile flowers,
Elder flowers,
Horseradish,
Lemon balm,
Linden flowers,
Saffron,
Sage,
Valerian,
Wormwood.

Diuretic

Increases the secretion and flow of urine.

Alder bark
Asparagus seed,
Balm of Gilead bark,
Birch leaves,
Black cohosh,
Bicorn tops,
Buchu leaves,
Burdock seeds,
Cleavers,
Cornsilk,
Dandelion root,
Elder flowers,
Goldenrod,
Horseradish,
Horsetail,
Juniper berries,
Lovage,
Parsley root,
Partridge berry,
Skunk cabbage,
Tansy,
Uva-Ursi,
Watermelon,
Yarrow.

Emetics

An agent that induces vomiting.

Bittersweet,
Bloodweed leaves,
Dwarf elder root,
Feber root,
Gentian root,
Mistletoe leaves,
Mustard seeds,
Yarrow,
Vervain,
Wood betony root.

Emmenagogue

Herbs that stimulate and normalize menstruation.

Black cohosh root,
Blood root,
Blue cohosh root,
Chamomile,
Cotton root,
Dandelion,
Figwort,
Linden,
Lungwort,
Parsley seeds,
Red raspberry,
Rosemary,
Rue,
Tansy,
Witch hazel,
Yarrow.

Emollient

Agent used to soften and soothe inflamed external area.

Chickweed,
Coltsfoot,
Elecampane root,
Flaxseed,
Garlic,
Mullein,
Onion,
Slippery elm bark.

Expectorants

Herbs that loosen phlegm of the mucous membranes and help to expel same.

Anise seeds,
Black cohosh root,
Coltsfoot,
Comfrey root,
Elder flowers,
Fennel,
Flaxseed,
Garlic,
Horehound,
Horseradish,
Lungwort
Mullein,
Onion,
Pleurisy root,
Sage leaves,
Spikenard.

Febrifuge

Remedy which helps to reduce fevers.

Blood root,
Boldo leaves,
Boneset,
Borage,
Catnip,
Centaury,
Chamomile,
Coltsfoot,
Elder flowers,
Feverwort,
Quassia bark,
Wormwood,
White willow bark.

Hepatics

Herbs said to activate the liver.

Barberry bark,
Black cohosh,
Cleavers,
Culver's root,
Dandelion root,
Elder,
Indian apple root,
Liverwort,
Mandrake root,
Plantain,
Uva-Ursi,
Wahoo bark,
Yarrow.

Herpatics

Herbs used for skin diseases (all kinds).

Bittersweet,
Borage,
Burdock,
Chickweed,
Comfrey,
Golden seal,
Myrrh,
Oleander leaves,
Onion,
Red clover,
Spikenard,
Yellow dock.

Lithotriptics

Herbs said to dissolve calculi (stones or gravel) in the urinary organs.

Black currant,
Buchu,
Cornsilk,
Parsley,
Sorrel,
Uva-Ursi,
Water plantain leaves.

Mucilages

Herbs that soothe inflammations (Gummy substance).

Buckhorn root,
Chickweed,
Comfrey,
Fenugreek seed,
Flaxseed,
Iceland moss,
Irish moss,
Lungwort,
Okra,
Slippery elm bark.

Nephritics

Herbs said to be useful in kidney disorders.

Black cohosh,
Blessed thistle,
Buchu leaves,
Chamomile flowers,
Cornsilk,
Couchgrass,
Gravel plant,
Irish moss,
Juniper berries,
Parsley root,
Partridge berry,
Poke root,
Queen of the meadow,
Uva-Ursi,
Yarrow.

Nervines

Herbs used to calm nerves and relieve tension.

Black cohosh root,
Blue skullcap,
Burdock seeds,
Catnip,
Celery seed,
Chamomile,
Garlic,
Hop flowers,
Hyssop,
Mullein,
Onion,
Parsley,
Peony root,
Rosemary leaves,
Squaw vine,
Valerian root,
Vervain.

Pectorals

Herbs used for relieving chest complaints.

Black horehound,
Borage,
Coltsfoot,
Comfrey root,
Eucalyptus,
Fennel,
Garlic,
Gentian,
Horseradish,
Jamaica ginger,
Licorice,
Lungwort,
Mullein,
Mustard,
Onion.

Soporifics

Agents that tend to induce sleep.

Catnip,
Elder flowers,
Hop flowers,
Scullcap,
Valerian,
Vervain,

Stimulants

Herbs used to increase functional activity on a general basis.

Allspice,
Balm of Gilead bark,
Black pepper,
Blood root,
Boldo leaves,
Cassia bark,
Garlic,
Gentian root,
Ginseng,
Horseradish,
Jamaica ginger,
Mustard,
Nutmeg,
Onion,
Rosemary.

Stomachic

Used to strengthen stomach and promote digestion.

Angelica root,
Anise seed,
Bay leaves,
Cardamom,
Celery seed,
Chamomile flowers,
Coriander seeds,
Dandelion root,
Fennel,
Horsemint leaves,
Lovage,
Nutmeg,
Peppermint,
Wormwood.

Styptics

Herbs used to stop bleeding (externally).

Bayberry,
Comfrey,
Grapevine leaves,
Life-Everlasting,
Matico leaves,
Nettle leaves,
Plantain,
Witch Hazel,
Yellow dock root.

Sudorific

Used to induce sweating

American Pennyroyal,
Anise seed,
Blessed thistle,
Blue cohosh root,
Boneset,
Burdock root,
Cayenne,
Cleavers,
Elder flowers,
Garlic,
Hyssop,
Sage.

Tonic

A substance used to strengthen and invigorate the system.

Alder,
American columba root,
Angelica root,
Anise seed,
Black alder bark,
Blackberry root,
Buchu leaves,
Chicory root,
Cleavers,
Comfrey,
Cornsilk,
Dandelion root,
Garlic,
Gentian root,
Ginseng root,
Golden seal,
Juniper berries,
Licorice,
Parsley,
Red raspberry,
Yellow dock.

Vermifuge

Used to expel worms from the system.

Blue flag root,
Buckthorn,
Culver's root,
Dulse,
Flaxseed,
Garlic,
Hyssop,
Mandrake root,
Onion,
Pumpkin seeds,
Red mulberry,
Senna leaves,
White oak,
Wormwood.

PREPARATION OF HERBS

Herbs are prepared in many different ways for use as medicine. When you receive your herbs for storage, be sure to enclose them in dark, airtight containers. Exposure to light can destroy the potency of the plants and this is often the reason that the desired results are not obtained. Cleanliness is also very important. Bacteria can easily be a problem if absolute care is not taken. When producing mixtures, make sure surfaces and utensils are spotlessly clean.

Infusion

This is actually a tea made by combining 1 oz. of the dried herb to 16 oz. of boiling water and allowing to steep for approximately 10 minutes. This is the way the virtues of the herbs are extracted. Strain the infusion into a container. When ready to drink (usually warm) sip slowly in small regular amounts, 4 oz. at a time, throughout the day (morning, noon and night). Honey may be added as a sweetener unless health reasons forbid sweetening. A dash of lemon is also good for taste.

Decoction

Barks, roots and seeds need more heating to extract the valuable ingredients. This is done by boiling ½ oz. plant to 8 oz. water, preferably in an earthenware pot (never metal), for approximately 15 minutes. Let cool, strain and drink by the wineglass, three or four times daily. If using green plants — add to cold water and bring to a boil and leave for five minutes, let steep, strain and serve. Dosage is always hard to determine because of plant freshness. Growing your own is the ideal — otherwise buy from a reputable source.

Steaming

Where steaming is recommended put a tablespoon of herbs into a medium sized bowl. Pour in bowling water, put a towel over the head and bowl (be careful not to burn yourself) and let the steam penetrate. This is a good way to clean bronchial problems and also is used to steam and cleanse the skin. If a very young child needs to clear the bronchial tubes, it is safer to use a steamer designed for that purpose — just add required herbs in the dispenser attached to the steamer, such as wintergreen. Another point to remember is that these preparations can go rancid. If in doubt never use, it doesn't take long to make a new batch.

Poultice

Poultices are used in several different ways. They are applied externally to either soothe, stimulate or draw poison from wounds. They should be applied warm and moist and checked often to make sure there is no irritation. When applying something as stimulating as a mustard plaster — make sure there is something between the skin and mustard as it can give a burn. Cheesecloth is good for use as it is soft against the skin. Crush the plants to be used and mix with something wet and warm such as bread and milk or slippery elm, apply directly and wrap something around it to keep the heat in. The following list gives alternatives.

Soothing Poultice

Bread and milk, flaxseed, cornmeal, slippery elm, bran, hops.

Stimulating Poultice

Boiled carrots, mustard.

Drawing Poultice

Yeast, cornmeal, honey.

Fomentations

Make an infusion or decoction — soak a wash-cloth or towel in it and apply hot to the affected part. Another method is to put the herbs in a bag — steep in the hot water — wring out and apply. This method holds the heat longer.

Ointments

Melt the base of the ointment to be used (lard or vaseline). Chop fresh herbs or grind dried ones to powder if desired. Stir into the fat and cook slowly until leaves feel crisp. Strain off fat, it will be green. Use as needed. Use one part herb to a few parts base. These are to be applied externally.

Poultice

Whatever substance is being used for a poultice, bread and milk, onion, or herbs, pour just enough boiling water over to make a hot mush. Place between two pieces of cloth and apply directly.

Syrups

Make a solution of honey and water. (8 oz. boiling water to 16 oz. honey) bring back to boil, remove and add to the infusion (tea) and bottle. This is an excellent way for the children to take unpleasant tasting teas.

Tincture

Some herbs need something stronger than water to extract their vital ingredients. Tinctures are therefore an excellent way to prepare these herbs.

Take fresh or dried herbs, chop and pound and add to 1 oz. of herb, 2 oz. water and 2 oz. alcohol. Allow mixture to stand in a bottle for approximately 10 days (preferably in a cool, dry place).

How To Make Up A Formula

The question is often asked — how do I know how much of each herb to use when making a formula? Generally formulas are divided into six parts as follows.
First Part — Three Active Herbs,
Second part — One Part Aromatic
Third part — One Part Demulcent,
Fourth part — One Part Laxative.
If you wish to make an Anti-Spasmodic, you would choose three herbs from that section and one from each of the others listed. You can use weight as a measurement, e.g. 1 oz. each of three active herbs and 1 oz. of each of the others. Sometimes the laxative is not used.

Sample Formula

1 oz. Linden flowers
1 oz. Mullein leaves
1 oz. Hops
1 oz. Fennel
1 oz. Flaxseed
1 oz. Senna

Equipment Needed To Prepare And Store Herbs

Strainer
Measuring cups
Dark airtight containers
Scale
Pestle and mortar
Seed grinder
Mesh screens for drying
Mason jars for sprouting
Dark bottles for tinctures
Cheesecloth (for Poultices)
Wooden chopping board

There is no need to spend a lot of money on containers and equipment to prepare and store herbs. Large jars with airtight caps can be painted brown and a picture of the herb it contains on the outside. This looks most attractive.

VITAMINS

Vitamins are necessary to maintain good health and prevent disease. The body is composed of billions of cells each made up of chemical elements. These cells are constantly being replaced by new ones and the old ones discarded. In order to replace the cells, new material is needed. We derive this material from the nutrients we take from food, vitamins and minerals. If we are consuming devitalized foods, this is the material the new cells will be made from. It is vitally important that we eat a balanced healthy diet, abundant in the life-giving properties found in nature's storehouse, vegetables and fruit. Balance seems to be the key to good health — vitamins and minerals found in plant life are balanced as they should be and, for that reason they should make up a large part of our diet. Knowing the vitamin and mineral content of different foods gives us a guildeline to follow — a good variety of foods properly prepared builds healthy bodies. Unless one has serious digestive problems approximately 50-75% of our diet should be raw.

In this chapter on vitamins, I have included foods that are not considered herbs but are high in vitamins, minerals, and protein.

Vitamin A

This is a fat soluble vitamin that can be stored by the body. Because it is insoluble in water, it does not deteriorate during cooking if care is taken to use airtight pans. Vitamin A is essential for general health but in particular it helps to prevent night blindness. Surprisingly enough, although Vitamin A is found in abundance in North America through adequate vegetables, dairy products, etc. many people suffer each year from a deficiency. There are two sources of Vitamin A, carotene, which is from vegetables and retinol from animals. There is indication that retinol taken in excessive amounts can cause toxic side effects such as headache, nausea, blurred vision and diarrhea. The recommended daily allowance is 5000 I.U. for an adult, although this may increase if advised by your physician during pregnancy. Sometimes when eating an abundance of vegetables high in carotene, the palms of the hands may turn a little yellow. This in itself is not harmful, just colorful. The following chart gives food sources of Vitamin A, also deficiency symptoms and functions.

DEFICIENCY SYMPTOMS

Night blindness. Sensitivity to light. Dry, itchy eyes. Scaly, dry skin and hair. Poor teeth and nails. Lack of appetite. Frequent colds. Dryness of mucous membranes. Allergies. Falling hair. Diarrhea.

USES

Builds resistance to infections. Promotes growth generally, especially in children. Helps to prevent formation of gall and kidney stones. Aids tooth and bone formation.

FOOD SOURCES

Carrots, dandelion greens, sorrel, kale, sweet potatoes, turnip greens, mustard greens, beet greens, collard, parsley, spinach, alfalfa, cress, broccoli, fennel, lettuce, endive, green onions, acorn squash, canteloupe. Asparagus, ripe tomatoes, rutebaga, elderberries, brussel sprouts, avocado, okra, cucumber, celery, peas, loganberries, blackberries, raspberries, peaches, guava, bananas. Apples, cranberries, grapes, grapefruit, lemons, limes, oranges, pears, pineapple, cauliflower, eggplant.

Vitamin B-1

Thiamine

The daily requirement of vitamin B-1 varies according to the calorie intake. It is necessary to convert carbohydrates into glucose which is used by the body as energy. As the carbohydrates are increased the need for B-1 increases also. Remember to keep cooking temperatures low, as high heat affects the B-1 content of foods. Prolonged deficiency can result in beri-beri which is a disease of the nerves and causes a paralysis of the limbs. For prevention of this disease, a diet rich in whole natural grains is necessary. Vitamin B-1 occurs in nature in a wide variety of foods, but whole grains seem to be the best source.

USES

General well being, prevents beri-beri, aids digestion and assimilation, improves appetite, nerve conditions and alcoholism, smokers, pregnancies, diabetics and hypothyroid conditions.

DEFICIENCY SYMPTOMS

Poor appetite, depression, digestive disturbance, shortness of breath, constipation, nervousness, craving for sweets, irritability, dry skin, burning in hands and feet, anemia.

FOOD SOURCES

Wheat germ, brown rice, rice bran, brewer's yeast, cereal grains (whole), nuts and seeds, peas and beans, asparagus, avocado, broccoli, cauliflower, chard, carrots, celery, dandelion greens, eggplant, figs, garlic, kale, mushrooms, parsley, spinach, tomato, apple, cantaloupe, grapefruit, honeydew, orange, pear, papaya.

Vitamin B-2

Riboflavin

The function of riboflavin is involved in the breakdown and utilization of carbohydrates, fats and proteins. It works very closely with the other B vitamins, especially thiamine and niacin. B-2 is soluable in water and although it is not affected too much by moderate heat, it is easily destroyed by light. There are many signs of B-2 deficienty, the most common are cracks and wrinkles around the lips and mouth corners.

USES

Promotes energy, good nerves, healthy skin, good digestion and elimination, helps to retain youthfulness.

DEFICIENCY SYMPTONS

Poor digestion, swollen eyelids, bloodshot eyes, red, sore tongue, dizziness, general debility, anemia, weight-control, shingles.

FOOD SOURCES

Wheat germ, dairy products, brewer's yeast, molasses, seeds, nuts, soybeans, asparagus, avocado, broccoli, mushrooms, dandelion greens, beet greens, artichockes, comfrey leaves, cabbage, celery, collards, turnip greens, spinach, Brussels sprouts, eggplant, grapefruit, orange, pears.

Vitamin B-3

Niacin

This is another member of the B family (these B's all work together) essential for the correct function of the intestinal tract (like B-1 and B-2). Acute deficiency of B-3 can cause pellagra (rough skin). This disease used to be common in the southern United States due to a lack of fresh vegetables and dairy products in the diet. Poor people lived mainly on a diet of hominy grits and deficiencies resulted. For prevention of B related diseases a balanced diet providing whole grains, dairy products, fresh fruits and vegetables is essential.

USES
Mental weakness, prevention of pellagra, circulatory problems, alcoholism, retarded growth.

DEFICIENCY SYMPTONS
Mental depression, irritability, insomnia, aches and pains, digestive disorders.

FOOD SOURCES
Wheat germ, brewer's yeast, rice polishings, green vegetables, dairy products, nuts and seeds, mushrooms, beans, alfalfa, parsley, dandelion greens.

Vitamin B-6

Pyridoxine

Vitamin B-6 is water soluble and is measured in milligrams. It is very necessary for the proper assimilation of protein and fat. It also is requred for the production of red blood cells. When grains are refined much of the B-6 is lost. It is therefore important to balance the diet with other sources of B-vitamins. If Vitamin B supplements are taken, make sure they are balanced as they work together as a family. B-1, B-2 and B-6 should be in equal amounts. Be careful not to use high heat in cooking grains — this destroys the B-6. A diet high in protein also needs supplemental B-6.

USES
Aids digestion, water retention, needed for production of red blood cells, skin problems.

DEFICIENCY SYMPTOMS
Anemia, irritability, mental depression, sore tongue, dizziness, nausea.

FOOD SOURCES
Wheat germ, brewer's yeast, whole grain cereals. spinach, broccoli, asparagus, cabbage, cantaloupe, dandelion greens.

Vitamin B-12

Cabolomin

This vitamin is necessary for the regeneration of red blood cells. It promotes growth generally and helps to prevent anemia. B-12 is measured in mcg. and is water soluble. Since B-12 is plentiful in dairy products and organ meats it is unlikely that a deficiency exists if these foods are consumed on a regular basis. Some people have a problem with absorption though, and this can lead to an anemic condition. Since the B-vitamins are so important for an overall feeling of well-being, a varied diet containing the complete B-complex is recommended since they all work together. Pregnant women usually need more and should consult their physician for a suggested amount. Women using birth control pills would also benefit from B-12.

USES

Increases energy level, improves concentration and appetite, prevents anemia, helpful for skin problems, promotes growth, hypoglecemia.

DEFICIENCY SYMPTOMS

Extreme fatigue, anemia, confused mentally, general run down feeling.

FOOD SOURCES

Organ meats, eggs, milk, cheese, yogurt, yeast, wheat germ, mushrooms, nuts, beans, comfrey leaves, cabbage.

Vitamin B-15

Panagamic Acid

There is much research to be done on B-15 to establish a true value for it. There is indication, however, that it helps to regulate fat metabolism and stimulates the nervous system. It is considered useful in the treatment of weak muscles and overall general debility. Since it is believed to extend the lifespan of the cells, some authorities claim it is an anti-aging factor.

USES
Stimulates nervous system, regulates fat metabolism, prevents premature aging.

DEFICIENCY SYMPTOMS
May cause glandular and nervous disorders.

FOOD SOURCES
Yeast, whole grains, nuts, seeds, rice, bran.

Vitamin B-17

Laetrille

The controversy still continues over this vitamin. It is being used legally by several States in America to treat cancer. The Food and Drug administration, however, still rejects it as a useful medicine and even contends it is poisonous because of the cyanide content. The food sources of this vitamin are found in the seeds of apricots, apples, buckwheat, peaches and flaxseed.

Other B Compounds

Pantothenic Acid

USES
Maintains normal skin growth, helps digestion and the building of body cells, calms nerves, promotes healthy skin.

DEFICIENCY SYMPTOMS
Painful burning feet, digestive disturbances, irritability, muscular weakness, hair loss, fatigue, depression, headaches.

FOOD SOURCES
Brewer's yeast, molasses, soybeans, wheat germ, egg yolks, organ meats, broccoli, carrots, cantaloupe, raw cabbage, watercress, mushrooms, celery, strawberries.

P.A.B.A. (Paraamino benzoic acid)

USES
Promotes growth generally, helps prevent grey hair, good for skin eruptions and alleviates fatigue, prevents sunburn in ointments.

DEFICIENCY SYMPTOMS
Extreme tiredness, irritability, headaches, depression, wrinkled skin.

FOOD SOURCES
Whole grains, wheat germ, organ meats, brown rice, bran, liver, legumes, brewer's yeast, molasses.

Folic Acid

USES
Helps formation of red blood cells, aids protein metabolism, stimulates hair growth, increases energy.

DEFICIENCY SYMPTOMS
Anemia, hair loss, skin disorders, mental depression.

FOOD SOURCES
Dark green leafy vegetables, nuts, soybeans, yeast, wheat germ, asparagus, broccoli, cabbage, carrots cauliflower, celery, cucumber, onions, mushrooms, peppers, avocado, bananas, grapes, grapefruit, oranges, pineapple, strawberries, watermelon, dairy products.

Biotin B-7

Biotin is measured in mcg. and is water soluble. It is essential for normal metabolism of protein and fat and usually works in conjunction with other members of the B family. There is indication that a deficiency can occur if raw egg whites are consumed daily since a substance found in the whites called avidin prevents Biotin absorption. It is destroyed by exposure to air in cooking but not by heat.

USES
Prevents skin problems (eczema, dermatitis), promotes normal metabolism of protein and fat, helps prevent grey hair.

DEFICIENCY SYMPTONS
Dry skin, eczema, dermatitis, loss of hair.

FOOD SOURCES
Brewer's yeast, nuts, organ meats, seeds, brown rice.

Choline

One of the lipotrophic factors necessary for normal fat metabolism, it is present in all living cells of the body. Choline needs Inositol to be effective but since it is widely found in unrefined foods it is hardly likely a deficiency exists if a balanced diet is consumed.

USES
Lowers cholesterol, helps to detoxify the liver. Good kidney function.

DEFICIENCY SYMPTOMS
Hardening of the arteries, high blood pressure.

FOOD SOURCES
Brewer's yeast, wheat germ, lecithin granules, sunflower seeds, egg yolks, liver, fish, green leafy vegetables.

Inositol

Inositol combines with choline to form lecithin and metabolizes fats in the body. Like choline it helps to control cholesterol build up and helps prevent gall bladder problems. It is measured in mgs. and is water soluble. Care must be taken in food preparation not to allow too much air exposure.

USES
Helps prevent eczema, lowers cholesterol level, aids fat metabolism, weight control.

DEFICIENCY SYMPTOMS
High cholesterol, eczema, hair loss.

FOOD SOURCES
Liver, soybeans, brewer's yeast, molasses, lecithin, cantaloupe, grapefruit, cabbage.

Vitamin C

This is probably the best known of all the vitamins since so much is written about it. Vitamin C is not stored by the body and unless an adequate intake from food is supplied constantly a deficiency can occur due to environmental conditions. Vitamin C is important for the formation of collagen (this is part of the connective tissue that cements body cells together). When collagen breaks down, sagging takes place and causes aging. It is essential for healthy blood vessels and needed for all tissue repair (especially bones and teeth). Vitamin C is taken by many people as a preventative against infection as well as for stress caused by anxiety. Smokers need more C as each cigarette destroys 25 mg. Air pollution also takes its toll. Vitamin C is needed for good skin and also the prevention of kidney stones. The list is endless, but one thing is certain — your body cannot function properly without it. Study the following chart and include adequate variety to your meals. If taking Vitamin C supplements be sure to take the natural source (rose hips, acerola, green peppers) as these contain the bioflavanoids needed for proper assimilation.

USES
Promotes healing, builds resistance to infection, builds healthy bones and teeth, maintains healthy skin especially good for collagen, breaks down cholesterol, helps prevent colds.

DEFICIENCY SYMPTOMS
Scurvy, fragile bones, bleeding gums, bruise easily, broken capillaries, slow to heal, low cold resistance, loss of appetite, anemia.

FOOD SOURCES
Citrus fruits, green leafy vegetables, tomatoes, berries, red pepper, cabbage, sprouts, broccoli, cauliflower, spinach, parsley, collard greens, kale, alfalfa, watercress, Brussels sprouts, mustard greens.

Vitamin D

This is known as the sunshine vitamin since exposure to the sun actually enables the body to produce Vitamin D. The responsibility of this vitamin is to build strong healthy bodies (especially in children) and to regulate the use of calcium and phosphorus in the body. Even if adequate calcium is taken, a lack of D can prevent absorption into the bone structure and a disease known as rickets can result. It is a very sad sight to see a badly deformed body (bow legs) as a result of Vitamin D deficiency. Like Vitamin A, Vitamin D is stored by the liver so adequate sun exposure in summer can help to provide winter needs with some help from the diet. During world war II in England cod liver oil was given to babies free of charge to ensure an adequate A - D supply.

USES
Provides energy, bone and teeth, formation, calcium regulator, nerve relaxer.

DEFICIENCY SYMPTOMS
Rickets (soft bones), tooth decay, retarded growth, muscular weakness and cramps, nervousness.

FOOD SOURCES
Fish liver oils, egg yolks, milk, butter, bonemeal, salmon, sardines, onions, garlic, kelp, watercress.

Vitamin E

This fat soluble vitamin is found in abundance in vegetable oils and leafy greens. It is measured in international units and is stored by the body but only for a short time. The processing and refining of food destroys the Vitamin E content so care is needed in the preparation. Extreme temperatures also affect it such as heat and extreme cold. Many claims have been made for Vitamin E and research is still going on. Some doctors have used it with success in treating heart problems and as an aid in preventing miscarriages. It is considered by some to be an anti-aging factor as well as a good source of energy. It is a wise idea for anyone taking Vitamin E in supplement form to have their blood pressure checked as it has been known to raise it in certain individuals. With an adequate diet it is unlikely that a deficiency exists as North Americans have access to a wide range of foods high in Vitamin E.

USES
Prevention of heart problems, burns, leg ulcers, varicose veins, supplies oxygen to the cells, anti-aging, increases circulation, treats scar tissue, (internally and externally).

DEFICIENCY SYMPTOMS
Sterility, constant miscarriages, fatigue, retarded growth, muscle degeneration, impotency, dry dull hair.

FOOD SOURCES
Wheat germ, vegetable oils, soybeans, whole grains, leafy greens, lettuce, sunflower seeds, almonds, eggs, alfalfa, linseed, cress, lentils, parsley, dandelion greens, sprouts.

Vitamin F

Commonly called unsaturated fatty acids, it is especially important for the utilization of saturated fat. Vegetable oils such as safflower, sunflower and peanut contain these essential acids. The need for Vitamin F seems to increase during the wintertime when the hair, skin and nails seem to become more brittle. There is also evidence that Vitamin F in the form of lecithin (derived from soybeans) helps to burn off adipose tissue and encourages weight loss.

USES
Burns fat, helps prevent cholesterol, aids weight reduction, improves skin and hair.

DEFICIENCY SYMPTOMS
Dry flaky skin, dry hair, eczema.

FOOD SOURCES
Wheat germ oil, soybeans, peanuts, sunflower seeds, pecans, almonds, avocado, greens, alfalfa.

Vitamin K

It is very unlikely if a well rounded diet is followed that a deficiency exists. Vitamin K is fat soluble and measured in mcg. It is essential for the formation of prothrombin — a necessary substance for the clotting of blood. The taking of synthetic Vitamin K supplements is considered dangerous by some authorities due to a build up in the blood that can cause a form of anemia. Vitamin K in its natural state (food) is the best way to take it.

USES
For normal clotting of blood, checks excessive menstruation.

DEFICIENCY SYMPTOMS
Hemorrhages resulting from prolonged blood clotting time. Bruising easily, tender gums.

FOOD SOURCES
Eggs yolks, soybean oil, green leafy vegetables, whole grains, alfalfa, parsley.

MINERALS

Vitamins generally are given more attention than minerals, but that does not mean they are more important. To be healthy, the body needs balance, so it is necessary to be aware of mineral needs since they do work together with vitamins. Trace minerals are present in the body in minute amounts, macrominerals which include calcium and phosphorus are present in higher quantities. The question often arises how much of each is needed to keep healthy? It seems again to point to correct balance by means of proper diet. The body functions more efficiently when slightly on the alkaline side — unfortunately North Americans generally consume too many acid producing foods because of high protein diets rather than a diet composed of fruits and vegetables (alkaline). When an imbalance occurs mineral deficiencies can appear. The following chart contains the minerals necessary for good health plus the foods that contain them. Nature is an excellent chemist — by studying the chart, it is possible to ensure adequate mineral supply. The key is assimilation and live fresh fruits and vegetables which contain enzymes that aid the absorption of the nutrients.

Calcium

Calcium is one of the most important minerals in the body since it is needed for the formation of strong bones and teeth. It is also utilized in other areas of the body where needed and promotes regular function of the heart muscle. There is indication that certain foods deplete the body of calcium. Chocolate is one of the worst offenders. Children and pregnant mothers may have to increase their calcium supply as their needs increase. Although almost all of the calcium content in the body is found in the bones and teeth, it is still essential to the rest of the body for the normal clotting of blood and the building of nerve tissue. Calcium absorption relies on adequate Vitamin D in the system.

USES
Maintains and builds healthy bones and teeth, aids blood clotting, strengthens heart muscle, calms nerves, insomnia, increases mental alertness, depression, menstrual cramps.

DEFICIENCY SYMPTOMS
Stunted growth, brittle bones, poor teeth, insomnia, cramps, irritability, poor circulation.

FOOD SOURCES
Dairy products, meat, fish, nuts, seeds, cheese, cabbage, onions, cauliflower, carrots, leeks, sprouts, dandelion greens, asparagus, kale, lettuce, spinach, broccoli, watercress, green leafy vegetables, oranges, lemons, grapes.

Chlorine

Chlorine plays an important part in controlling body fluids and is a general cleanser of the body. It also helps to reduce fat. Chlorine is closely related to sodium and if a deficiency exists in one it usually is related to the other. Balance is important in controlling body fluids and too much salt added to the diet can upset this. Most raw natural vegetables contain adequate amounts of salt but unfortunately North Americans like to add extra salt for taste and this can lead to water retention problems as well as high blood pressure.

USES
Reduces fat, aids digestion, body cleansing, keeps joints supple.

DEFICIENCY SYMPTOMS
Digestive disorders, joint stiffness, aches and pains, bloating.

FOOD SOURCES
Meats, egg yolk, asparagus, cabbage, cucumber, lettuce, watercress, spinach, tomatoes, kale, Swiss chard, radish, olives, dandelion greens, peas, onions, celery.

Copper

Copper works closely with iron and the body's requirements are small. If adequate iron is supplied it is hardly likely that a copper deficiency exists.

USES
Needed for iron assimilation to prevent anemia, helps Vitamin C utilization.

DEFICIENCY SYMPTOMS
Anemia, impaired respiration, digestive problems, low blood pressure.

FOOD SOURCES
Whole grains, molasses, liver, nuts, apricots, green leafy vegetables, broccoli, leeks, parsley, lettuce, cabbage, all berries.

Iron This mineral is necessary and essential for the production of hemoglobin (red pigment of blood cells). A steady supply is needed by the cells for life-supporting oxygen. Iron, then, is of vital importance. Women lose a certain amount each month and this has to be replaced or a deficiency can and often does occur. Anyone who has suffered from an iron deficiency can tell of the fatigue, irritability and shortness of breath. British studies have shown women in their pre-menstrual phase suffer from a variety of symptoms — from depression to violence. Adequate nutrition during this time may alleviate these prob lems. Many of the inorganic iron supplements on the market cause constipation. There are some preparations however based on natural ingredients which eliminate this problem. A well balanced diet will certainly help with your iron supply — study the chart and use a good variety.

USES
Increases energy, helps in development of red blood cells, prevents anemia and fatigue, aids growth.

DEFICIENCY SYMPTOMS
Fatigue, anemia, shortness of breath, sore tongue, irritability, depression.

FOOD SOURCES
Liver, kidney, egg yolks, figs, prunes, apricots, dates, raisins, peanuts, walnuts, molasses, whole-wheat, rice, bran, beet tops, chard, watercress, parsley, dandelion greens, spinach, cabbage, broccoli, burdock root, nettle leaves, kelp, Irish moss.

Iodine Iodine is needed by the thyroid gland to produce a hormone known as thyroxin, which affects mental and physical development. Iodine deficiency can cause hypothyroidism (under-secretion of thyroxin), and an enlargement of the glands commonly called a goitre can occur. Overweight sometimes is an indication of a thyroid problem and if this condition exists in spite of a controlled diet a physical checkup may be needed. Constantly cold hands and feet can also be an indication. People living inland are more apt to suffer a lack of iodine that our neighbours by the sea.

USES
Aids thyroid, increases energy, controls weight, prevents goitre, aids circulation.

DEFICIENCY SYMPTOMS
Dry skin and hair, goitre, overweight, mental fatigue, cold extremities, skin problems.

FOOD SOURCES
Seafood, kelp, dulse, watercress, Irish moss, endive, asparagus, nettle, cabbage, celery, parsley, spinach, cucumber, garlic, broccoli, apples, oranges, pears, figs, berries.

Magnesium

The majority of magnesium in the body is found combined with calcium in the bone structure. It is also contained in muscles and soft tissue and is essential for the nerves. It is very unusual to find a deficiency if an adequate diet of whole grains, vegetables, nuts and seeds is supplied, but it is not unusual for alcoholics and refined food eaters to suffer from lack of this mineral.

USES
Builds healthy nerves, prevents stress, helps muscles, prevents formation of gallstones, prevents constipation.

DEFICIENCY SYMPTOMS
Brittle bones, nervousness, depression, muscle twitches.

FOOD SOURCES
Soybeans, whole grains, almonds, peanuts, sunflower seeds, pecans, dairy products, oranges, lemons, grapefruit, apples, peaches, pears, dandelion greens, spinach, chard, beet greens, kale, onions, parsnips, turnip greens, broccoli, cauliflower, tomatoes.

Manganese

Manganese is measured in mg. and there is no R.D.A. for it, however, 2 to 5 mg. is generally accepted as the requirement for good health. It seems to be necessary as an activator for certain enzymes in the system and also as an aid to digestion. It also plays a part in blood formation.

USES
Increases mental capacity, calms nerves, strengthens eyes and bones.

DEFICIENCY SYMPTOMS
Depression, digestive problems, nervousness, fatigue, dizziness, swollen glands.

FOOD SOURCES
Dairy products, nuts, organ meats, fish, apples, lemons, grapefruit, grapes, parsley, lettuce, watercress, peas, endive, nettle, chives, nasturtium.

Phosphorus

This mineral functions along with calcium to form sound teeth and bones. It is present in every cell of the body and has many important functions such as cell repair and keeping hair and skin healthy. It is needed for proper utilization of fats and proteins thus providing the body with energy. People using their mental capacities certainly need adequate phosphorus since it nourishes the brain cells.

USES
Repairs cells, aids growth, promotes strong bones and teeth, improves mental capacity, provides energy.

DEFICIENCY SYMPTOMS
Retarded growth, weak nerves, poor teeth, brittle bones, mental fatigue, poor skin and hair.

FOOD SOURCES
Meat, dairy products, whole grains, sunflower seeds, sesame, soybeans, pumpkin seeds, citrus fruit, apples, grapes, berries, garlic, Irish moss, kale, Brussels sprouts, sprouts, parsley, watercress, spinach, beet greens, broccoli.

Potassium

Potassium is found in a wide variety of foods. It works very closely with sodium in the body to regulate the balance of fluids. Although potassium is plentiful in foods, certain conditions can cause a loss of this mineral — excessive intake of sugar, coffee and diuretics deplete the body of this mineral.

USES
Weight control, builds appetite, aids digestion and normal muscle function, helps heart function.

DEFICIENCY SYMPTOMS
May cause constipation, fatigue, lack of appetite, edema.

FOOD SOURCES
Molasses, lima beans, soybeans, citrus fruit, raspberries, strawberries, bananas, papaya, avocado, parsley, cress, chard, parsnip, garlic, spinach, mushrooms, cooked potato, peas, Brussels sprouts, dandelion greens, broccoli, kale, mustard greens, asparagus, chervil, cabbage, mint leaves, celery.

Silicon

This could well be labelled a beauty mineral since it is largely responsible for promoting healthy skin, nails and hair. If a deficiency exists it affects the whole nervous system which, in turn, can cause hair loss.

USES
Promotes healthy skin, hair and nervous system. General well-being.

DEFICIENCY SYMPTOMS
Loose gums, brittle nails, dull lifeless hair, hair loss, boils, itchy skin.

FOOD SOURCES
Strawberries, blueberries, lettuce, mustard greens, asparagus, parsnips, dandelion greens, chard, celery, cauliflower, spinach, collards, kale, cabbage, cucumber, leeks, oat straw, horsetail.

Sodium

It is hardly likely that a sodium deficiency exists in most people, in fact it is usually the reverse due to excessive use of table salt on food. Sodium is abundant in many vegetables, the best source of supply. Sodium controls the acid alkaline balance of the blood and aids in keeping calcium soluble.

USES
Keeps system alkaline, aids muscle function, aids digestion.

DEFICIENCY SYMPTOMS
Bloating, heat stroke, retarded growth, joint stiffness, general weakness.

FOOD SOURCES
Carrots, celery, turnips, beet greens, artichokes, dandelion greens, spinach, watercress, parsley, asparagus, Swiss chard, olives, kelp, Irish moss.

Sulphur

There is no R.D.A. for this mineral, but if a diet provides sufficient protein there is usually enough sulphur to supply needs. It is also considered as much a beauty mineral as silicon is because of its part in producing healthy skin, hair and nails. It is extremely cleansing to the system and builds natural resistance to infection.

USES
Promotes healthy skin, nails, hair, cleanses system, purifies blood.

FOOD SOURCES
Meat, fish, dairy products, nuts, oranges, apples, peaches, raspberries, rhubarb, Brussels sprouts, watercress, cabbage, cauliflower, spinach, parsnip, radish, cucumber, lettuce, carrot, dandelion greens, eggplant, shepherd's-purse, plantain leaves, chives.

Zinc

Although Zinc is found in most body tissues it is more concentrated in the sex glands. It is needed also for tissue repair and helps to maintain the body's acid-alkaline balance.

USES
Promotes general growth, helps maintain acid-alkaline balance, aids digestion.

DEFICIENCY SYMPTOMS
Retarded growth, prostate gland problems.

FOOD SOURCES
Nuts, beans, whole grains, dairy products, brewer's yeast, apples, oranges, cabbage, lettuce, carrot, onion, spinach, peas, pumpkin seeds.

HERBS AS BEAUTY AIDS

Throughout history both men and women have been interested in improving the way they look. Egypt is usually credited with starting the cosmetic trend. Women particularly used creams, powders, hair dyes and nail polish in great abundance. The ingredients they used for their cosmetics were from many different sources — some good, others quite dangerous. Henna was used to dye the hair, but lead derivatives were used to paint eyes and cheeks.

The Greeks and Romans contributed to cosmetology by introducing vegetable oils, honey and milk for keeping the skin supple. (Remember the movies about milk bathing). Our native Indians extracted beautiful colors from vegetables to paint their faces with, and the pioneers to the Americas also brought with them knowledge of herbs and their uses as beauty aids. I can remember as a child in England how sweet smelling my grandmother was — she always had a fragrance of either roses or lavender about her. I remember her saving the petals of flowers and making them into little sachets to put into the linen cupboard. I also know Gran used to wash her hair with herbs from the garden.

We probably have more selection today of beauty items than ever before, the question is how effective are they? Some advertising claims would have us believe we can look years younger by using this miracle cream or that rejuvenating lotion. Cosmetics are fun and people of all ages enjoy experimenting to see what improvement they can achieve. There is one drawback though — sometimes the ingredients in these products are not particularly healthy. Many

dermatologists I'm sure will confirm that some products actually cause dermatitis and allergic reactions that are difficult to clear up. Some women suffer more serious damage especially to the eyes and fingernails. Caustic ingredients used on delicate tissue is almost certain to cause a reaction.
For the past fifteen years I have been interested in natural skin care. By experimenting with herbs, fruits, vegetable oils and honey, etc. I honestly believe that nature's ingredients are superior to the man made synthetics. There are certain natural ingredients that can cause allergic reactions in some people, just as food can, but there doesn't seem to be the danger of actually causing serious tissue damage. If an allergy exists, just stop using it and try something else.
You will have fun using herbs (especially if you have grown them) for your beauty needs. Some will be more effective for you than others. One thing though — you certainly will have not spent a fortune and the results will be most gratifying.

Tips For A Healthy Skin

No matter what type of skin you have, dry, normal, oily or a combination, there are basic rules that apply to all of them to keep a balanced healthy glowing complexion.

(1) Diet — This should supply the body with valuable nutrients needed for rebuilding all tissue. It really does mean feeding your face — literally! Fresh vegetables and fruits, whole grains enough liquid and unsweetened juices, protein, a balanced and nutritious diet will give you a good start on a beautiful skin. (As important is what you don't eat — candy, chocolate, pop, excessive salt, sugar, potato chips), etc. Devitalized junk foods do very little to improve appearance (you get mostly empty calories). Remember the vitamins that feed the skin are A, B, C, D and E. Refer to chapter on vitamin content of foods.

(2) Elimination — A clean inside reflects on the outside. Proper elimination is vitally important for the complexion. Drinking 6 - 8 glasses of water each day will do much to flush the system. In our house we always say when you are green inside you are clean inside. (Eat lots of vegetables).

(3) Exercise — Apart from the obvious benefits to your figure — the skin also reacts well to good circulation. Daily exercise in the fresh air is very helpful. Good circulation means good color tone. Walking near the trees is an excellent way of getting clean air into your lungs — breathe deeply and think of how oxygen is taken through the blood to your skin.

(4) Relaxation — It is necessary to have adequate rest and feel relaxed. A strained tired body is usually reflected in the face causing

stress lines and wrinkles, especially around the eyes. When resting it is a good idea to have the feet higher than the head, this allows the blood flow to reverse.

(5) Cleanliness — Skin that looks dull and muddy is very unattractive. Cleansing the skin often to remove the dirt and grime that accumulates is extremely essential. It is probably the most important external ritual you do each day. If it is possible to cleanse 3 times daily — do it. You will see the results in a lively glowing skin. City dwellers especially need to do this. There is pollution floating around that settles into the pores of the skin causing blockages and eruptions — frequent washing helps (even if you have dry skin).

(6) Moisture — Keeping good moisture balance prevents the skin from drying out and becoming wrinkled. Both winter and summer are hard on the skin if precautions are not taken. Excessive sunbathing does much harm and speeds up the ageing process. If you do love to lie in the sun do so before noon and after 3 p.m. as the ultraviolet rays are less powerful at these times. Use a good sunscreen and be sure to apply lots of moisture afterwards. Wintertime is equally hard because of cold winds — the skin becomes chapped and irritated. If you love to ski pretend it is summer and apply a good sunscreen (reflection from snow is intense). Prevention is always better — have a routine of cleansing and moisturizing and stay with it faithfully.

Cleaners From Nature

Many cleansing creams available commercially actually clog the pores and are hard to remove — look to your kitchen for some effective products that cost very little. When using a cleanser it should serve several purposes, to clean, nourish and condition at the same time.

Dry To Normal Skin

- Avocado oil
- Apricot kernel oil
- Almond oil
- Peanut oil
- Sesame oil
- Buttermilk
- Yogurt
- Mayonnaise

Any of the above items are beneficial as a cleanser by themselves. If you want to try making a mixture of herbs with them, all the better Chamomile, elder flowers, comfrey, marigold flowers all help a dry skin. Make an infusion of 4 oz. boiling water to 1 oz. herb. Cool and strain. Take a small tub of plain yogurt or use mayonnaise — add herb liquid and mix well. Put into tight lid jar and refrigerate. Remember 1 Tbsp. Safflower oil taken internally twice daily really helps skin.

Oily Skin

- Corn oil
- Safflower oil
- Sunflower oil
- Buttermilk
- Yogurt

Anyone with an oily skin may wonder about the use of oils on skin that has too much to start with. The secret is just use a small amount (the size of a quarter in the palm of the hand) and use this for the whole face and neck area. Rinse off five or six times with tepid water and then take either a slice of cucumber, or a cotton ball dipped in a solution of apple cider vinegar and water (half and half) and rub into the skin. Heavy cleansing creams do little for an oily skin — buttermilk will do a good job and if you care to use an herb added (the same procedure as for dry skin), lemon grass, witch hazel, marigold, yarrow or rosemary, make a good cleanser.

Combination Skin

- Avocado oil
- Apricot
- Almond
- Safflower
- Sunflower
- Buttermilk
- Yogurt
- Mayonnaise

Sometimes a combination skin needs different treatment depending on how extreme the oily-dry areas are. Experiment with the above oils for cleansing and for herbs try some from both lists and find which is best for you. Certain herbs such as chamomile, elder flowers, marigold, comfrey and peppermint are good for all types of skin.

Steaming

Steaming the skin helps to remove ingrained dirt and blackheads, and acts as a general cleanser and moisturizer. If you have broken capillaries (usually on the nose or cheeks) cover these with taped on gauze as steaming is not recommended. I love to steam my skin at least once a week and find it brightens my complexion and gives it a nice glow. If you have dry, scaly areas and stubborn blackheads a good deep pore scrub using 1 Tbsp. cornmeal mixed with a little water and gently massaged over entire face does wonders. Put 2 Tbsp. of herbs in a large bowl — pour over boiling water (be careful not to burn yourself), make a tent with a large towel and put face over the steam for about 10 minutes.

Oily skin steam use — comfrey, lavender, yarrow, lemon grass, marigold, rosemary, witch hazel.

Dry skin — juniper, chamomile, peppermint, orange flowers, elder flowers.

Combination — experiment with both.

Facial Masks

Facial masks do much to enhance the complexion. There are so many ingredients in your kitchen that do a wonderful job, you really don't need to spend a lot of money at a commercial salon. You will not only save money, but you will also know exactly what you are putting on your skin. The following masks have been used with excellent results. Experiment and find out which does the most for you. Once a mask is on your face, lie down and relax. Soak a gauze in witch hazel or eyebright and put over the eyes — this gives you a chance to rejuvenate your eyes at the same time as your skin. Never put the mask directly around the eyes or the lips.

Dry Skin

Choose of one these.

(1) Mix one ripe banana with ½ tsp. olive oil — apply to skin and leave on 15 minutes.

(2) Take 1 Tbsp. brewer's yeast, ½ tsp. wheat germ oil, open 1 capsule of halibut liver oil. Mix altogether and apply to face, leave on 15 minutes. (This is an excellent treatment since it nourishes the skin.)

(3) Mash a ripe avocado — apply to skin — leave on 15 minutes.

(4) 2 Tbsp. cottage cheese
1 Tbsp. honey
1 Tbsp. yogurt

Stir together until well mixed — apply to skin and leave on 15 minutes. Rinse off several times with warm water.

(5) 1 beaten egg yolk
1 Tbsp. honey
1 Tbsp. chamomile tea.

This mask tends to draw — leave on 15 minutes.

(6) Mash ½ ripe papaya
1 tsp. olive oil
1 tsp. honey

Mix well and leave on 15 to 20 minutes. This takes away the layer of dead cells and leaves the skin so-o-o smooth.

Masks For Oily Skin (Choose one of these)

(1) The pulp of a raw tomato applied to face and left on 15 minutes acts as a mild dermabrasive, leaves oily skin very refreshed. Cucumber can be used the same way.

(2) Pat on plain buttermilk, leave on 15 minutes. Wash off with warm water. Splash on apple cider vinegar (diluted ½ and ½ with water) as a freshener.

(3) 2 Tbsp. plain yogurt to 3 ripe strawberries — mix well. Leave on skin for 15 minutes.

(4) Make an infusion of yarrow (3 oz. water to 1 Tbsp. herb), cool and strain. Beat an egg white until frothy, add 1 Tbsp. of tea and apply to face and neck. Leave on 15 minutes.

(5) Warm honey and gently apply to the face. This mask has drawing power and helps to bring out impurities. Leave on 15 minutes.

(6) Herbal infusions of lemon grass, white oak bark or witch hazel can be made (strong ones as in recipe 4) and a Tbsp. added to plain yogurt — this makes an effective mask that should be left on for 20 minutes.

Deep Pore Cleansers

If we were to look at our face through a powerful magnifying glass, we would notice old skin constantly shedding as new replaces it. To help this process along, a once weekly deep pore cleansing is very helpful. Take any abrasive such as oatmeal, ground almonds or apricot kernels, cornmeal, whole grains and mix a little into the palm of the hands with water to make a paste. Steam the skin first for 10 minutes then gently rub ground meal all over the face (you can always do the hands as well). This helps to slough off the dead cells and leaves the skin tingling and yet soft and fresh. (This is especially helpful for oily skin). If your skin is dry be sure to use moisture afterwards.

Moisturizers

The skin needs moisture to stay supple and soft and prevent wrinkles. The best time to apply any steam or oil is when you have cleansed your face and your skin is still slightly damp. Now comes the question — which type of moisturizer is better? Animal oils or vegetable based products? The answer is to experiment and see which is right for you. Apricot oil, avocado, safflower, olive, cocoa butter and safflower margarine all feel good on the skin. Lanolin, turtle oil and mink oil are also of benefit to some skins. Not everyone can use lanolin (from sheep). I personally like it because my skin is exceptionally dry whereas a friend of mine with oily skin simply cannot tolerate it. I've also found weather conditions do play a part in the condition of the skin. Wintertime is especially hard because of contrasts between outside and inside temperature and humidities — a heavier moisturizer seems to be needed at this time. Summertime a light oil such as apricot seems adequate and feels so good.

Eyes

There are many ways to keep eyes shining, clear and bright. The number one rule is to get lots of rest. Tired puffy eyes are certainly not very attractive. When lying in the tub, it is a good idea to soak gauze pads in a solution of witch hazel and place over the eyes. Cold tea bags of rose hips or chamomile help to reduce any puffiness around the eye area. An eyewash of eyebright or a pinch of salt in 8 oz. water does wonders to clear up bloodshot, tired eyes. Sesame or olive oil is effective as an eye make-up remover, and for the prevention of wrinkles, pat on vitamin E or apricot kernel oil every night. If you prefer to use herbs for darkening the eyelashes, rosemary or sage do an effective job. To increase growth for eyelashes, use castor oil nightly before retiring.

Hands And Feet

For dry rough hands or feet, take a slice of lemon or papaya and gently massage all over rough area. (Elbows and heels too). This helps to remove the dead cells and leaves the skin soft. Any vegetable oils such as olive, avocado, safflower, wheat germ, sesame, apricot, massaged into the hands is beneficial. Pure lanolin or cooking lard is also very good. Chamomile, comfrey, elder and marigold flowers can be added in the form of a strong infusion to an oil or cream base (use the same recipe as for face). Use your imagination and make up something of your own. Care should be taken in a preventative way.

(1) Always wear gloves to do manual work (dishes, gardening).
(2) When moisturizing face, include the hands.
(3) When using fruit for a meal (papaya, lemon, cucumber, avocado, use skins to wipe over the hands.
(4) Give hands a bath in oatmeal once a week. 8 oz. to ½ cup water — soak 10 minutes.

The feet shouldn't be neglected either — keep them healthy by wearing shoes that fit properly. Remove hard skin that forms — give a good oil massage at least once a week. Soaking feet in a footbath to which 1 pint rosemary tea (made with 3 Tbsp. leaves) has been added, leaves the feet very refreshed. Salt water is also effective to soothe away those aches and pains.

Hair

Since the hair is mainly protein, it makes sense that diet plays a large part in keeping it healthy. Fresh fruit, vegetables, nuts and seeds are foods with an abundance of vitamins and minerals. All are necessary for beautiful hair. External care is equally important — unfortunately the excessive use of dyes — harsh shampoos, chemicals and hair dryers shows up in dry, dull, split hair.

Tips for Good Hair Care

(1) Eat a balanced diet — eliminate devitalized foods.
(2) Stand on your head often to allow the blood flow to get to the scalp.
(3) Use natural bristle brush instead of synthetic one.
(4) Use mild shampoo.
(5) Put one tsp. wheat germ oil in with second shampoo, (even for oily hair — massage well into scalp).
(6) Give a good conditioning with each shampoo.
(7) Wash hair as often as it needs it.
(8) Make sure all shampoos is rinsed out of the hair, (especially coarse hair since it is quite porous).
(9) Have it trimmed regularly to remove split ends.

Chamomile has been used throughout the ages as a rinse for fair hair. It brings out the highlights and gives a wonderful sheen to the hair. For dark haired ladies, rosemary or sage will do the same. Just make an infusion of either one you need and give the hair a rinse through after the shampoo. If you are having problems with dry itchy scalp or dandruff, make a strong infusion of nettle and massage well into a damp scalp. This remedy really works and keeps scalp healthy. Aloe Vera can be used in the same way — in fact I have a friend who keeps a large Aloe Vera stem in readiness to use on her hair as a treatment at least once a week. (Yes, she has a wonderful head of hair). The herb most talked about for hair these days is Jojoba. Many people claim it thickens up the hair and even encourages growth. It seems to be rather an expensive oil but for people who have a problem with sparse hair it seems to be worth it. As a hair conditioner

— good old egg yolks have been proven to be one of the best, certainly this was a favourite of grandma's and many hairdressers I have spoken with assure me it really does work (and it's so inexpensive). For fun try using other herbal infusions as a rinse. Marigold, red sage, comfrey, mullein, white oak bark and red clover are some of the herbs used in many commercial products.

Nails

Many women complain about their nails splitting, ridging and peeling. It is very frustrating when your hair looks beautiful and shiny, your skin is fresh and glowing and your nails are a mess. Nails take a lot of abuse if we don't wear gloves while cleaning or gardening, etc. I know a delightful lady in her 80's who has lovely nails. Her secrets?

(1) Eat a diet rich in foods containing sulphur and silicon (see mineral chart) and eat adequate protein.
(2) Massage warm wheat germ or olive oil into nails (especially around the cuticle) twice weekly.
(3) Keep nails manicured so that old tissue is removed to allow for new growth.
(4) Scrub nails with a nail brush daily to increase circulation.
(5) Always massage hands with lanolin after washing to lubricate nails, as they get dried out, too.
(6) ALWAYS WEAR GLOVES TO WORK AROUND THE HOUSE.

Comfrey tea taken several times daily provides the body with adequate calcium to build healthy nails.

Teeth

Well cared for teeth certainly add to anyone's attractiveness. Regular visits to the dentist for repair work is not only essential for good looks but also to maintain good health. If the teeth are bad, mouth odor is usually present. Is there anything worse? There are many good herbal toothpastes available at your local health store. If you wish you can make up your own. Charcoal powder can be used and it does a super job of whitening the teeth. You can add a drop of pure peppermint oil for refreshing taste. Plain table salt and water mixed with baking soda (½ and ½) is also effective. A wash of salt and water does a wonderful job of keeping the gums healthy (don't swallow it though). Herbs make very effective mouthwashes that do not aggravate the membranes.

(1) 1 tsp sassafras with 8 oz. water. Boil together, cool and use to rinse mouth.

(2) Put 5 drops of pure peppermint oil to 2 oz. hot water.

(3) Chew parsley or cloves to freshen mouth, especially after eating onions or garlic.

(4) A few drops of liquid chlorophyll in water deodorizes the mouth and the rest of the body.

Diet is important for healthy teeth. Refined foods such as candy, soft drinks, potato chips, sugar products all help teeth decay.

Herbal Baths

There is no greater treat than a soak in the tub after a day at the office — especially if the water has a delightful fragrance and a softening effect on the skin. For some people a bath can mean a dry itchy skin for hours afterwards. There are many ways to prevent this by using herbs and oils that come right from your own kitchen. When taking a bath with herbs you have to decide if you feel like a relaxing or a stimulating tub — herbs each have a different effect. An herbal soak can also be used medicinally, for example, trying to rid the body of a cold. Make a strong infusion with sage, strain and pour into the tub. Sage makes the body perspire and helps the body rid itself of toxins. Go right to bed after your bath. Body rashes can be helped by taking an oatmeal bath. This softens the water and soothes the skin. This remedy is good for babies with diaper rash. For an aching body, nothing works as well as equal amounts of baking soda and seasalt, (½ cup of each) added to the bath water. This is healing as well as soothing. Notice how a dip in the ocean heals skin conditions?

Bath Bags

Obviously to throw a handful of herbs into the tub could play havoc with the drains as well as leaving a messy tub. Bath bags are very convenient as well as pretty. (They make lovely gifts), and they can be made ahead of time and kept in your linen cupboard until ready to use.

Take a square of material 7 inches by 6 inches (it could be pretty lace or cheesecloth or soft cotton) put a tablespoon of herbs (either one of a kind or a mixture) and tie it with a ribbon. If you leave a long tie you can hang the bag on the taps and allow the water to run through it into the tub. Another way is to make a strong infusion of the mixture you want, strain and add to bathwater. Check section on herbs for dry or oily skin and make up bath bags according to skin type. Sweet smelling herbs such as lavender, rose petals, lemon balm, cloves, basil, peppermint, chamomile can be used as a mixture or used separately to provide a delightful treat. Pine needles tied in muslin and allowed to float in the bathwater provides a very relaxing bath. Bath oils can be made at a tenth of the price of commercial products and are certainly healthier. If you have a dry skin lightly rub sesame oil all over before soaking in the tub, as this will allow you to stay in longer. Use Almond oil, Safflower, Sunflower oil, or Avocado oil with a little fragrance added (concentrated herbal oils are ideal) for an economical and healthy bath treat. Essential oils from plants can be expensive — only use one or two drops per bath. Since they are very concentrated that is all you will need. Your local health store and some pharmacies keep a good selection of these oils.

Sachets

Just recently, a friend gave me as a gift a basket filled with herbal sachets tied up with pretty ribbon. The bottom of the basket was filled with baby's breath and tucked away in one corner was a bar of herbal soap. The whole effect was so delightful (and practical) that I've decided to give these as gifts (birthday and Christmas) to my relatives and friends this year. What a wonderful project for the summer — gathering the herbs to be used and preparing them ahead of time until ready for making the sachets. It also gives ample time to experiment with different herbs and scents to see which is most appealing.

(1) Step 1. Collect the herbs you intend to experiment with.

Flowers and leaves. Rose petals, violets, chamomile, lavender, sage, lemon verbena, lemon balm, mint, dried orange or lemon rind.

(2) Mix altogether in a large crock or keep some separate if you wish. Leave one month or longer.

(3) Make your squares of cotton material 7" x 6" and place small handful of herbs in the centre. Gather up the edges together and secure with a pretty ribbon. Different kinds of materials can be used to give color, or opaque a see through fabric to show the color of the herbs. If lemon rind or orange is added the scent will stay potent longer.

Some herbs obviously have a stronger scent than others. For those that do not, the perfume has to develop over a period of time. Mix the herbs together as above and add a fixative such as gum benzoin or orris root (This helps to preserve the scents). Spices such as caraway, cinnamon, cloves, and anise can also be crushed and added to give added aroma. To measure fixative usually to 8 oz. herbs add ¼ tsp. — store for about 1 month in airtight containers, preferably pottery. These herbs can also be put into pretty jars and used to sweeten the smell of the air in the house. Use any herb that appeals to you — the list is endless! Pay a visit to a herb shop and get ideas. Above all have fun and enjoy the perfumes of nature. You can certainly be as creative and original as you wish.

INDEX